LOVE *to* PRAY

A 40-Day Devotional for Deepening Your Prayer Life

WITH A COMPANION GUIDE FOR GROUP STUDY

Dr. Alvin VanderGriend

PRAYERSHOP PUBLISHING

Terre Haute, Indiana
www.prayershop.org

PrayerShop Publishing is the publishing arm of Harvest Prayer Ministries and the Church Prayer Leaders Network. Harvest Prayer Ministries exists to make every church a house of prayer. Its online prayer store—www.prayershop. org—offers more than 400 prayer resources for purchase.

Cover design: Pamela Poll
Text design: Pamela Poll
Editor: Paul Faber

Published in cooperation with:
Alvin J. VanderGriend
606 Woodcreek Drive
Lynden, WA 98264

1 2 3 4 5 6 7 8 9 10 | 12 11 10 09 08 07

Introduction
to the New Edition

L ove to Pray: A 40-Day Devotional Guide for Deepening Your Prayer
Life was first published in 2003. Its popularity with small groups
and in education classes encouraged us to write a companion study
guide for groups that was used separately. In this new edition the 40-day
Love to Pray devotional and the eight-week study guide for groups are
combined.

Using *Love to Pray* by Itself
The *Love to Pray* devotional guide can be used independent of the study
guide. Individuals use the devotional guide for personal devotions to
deepen and strengthen their prayer lives. Families are using *Love to Pray*
for family devotions—a practice that stimulates spiritual growth, especially when family members participate in the "Reflect," "Pray," and "Act"
segments together. Prayer cells are using the devotional to enhance the
personal prayer lives of cell members and strengthen their intercessory
prayer ministries.

Using *Love to Pray* with the Study Guide
and Optional DVD
Small groups and church education classes are using the study guide with
Love to Pray to facilitate interactive learning and to encourage group
prayer. Each session in the study guide begins with an optional DVD
presentation by a prayer leader. (Available from PrayerShop Publishing.)
The "React" question in each lesson relates to the DVD presentation and
is intended to evoke a response and discussion. Groups work through

each study guide session by focusing on a key Scripture passage, responding to the inductive questions, and concluding with a prayer time.

Some groups use the study guide without the DVD presentation,
beginning their discussion with the "Share" question. In either case
participants are encouraged to read the *Love to Pray* devotional section
mentioned in the "Suggested Reading This Week" at the end of each
weekly session. These readings will reinforce what the group has learned
together.

Using *Love to Pray* in a *40 Days of Prayer* Initiative

40 Days of Prayer is a whole-church prayer initiative designed to help
churches become "devoted to prayer." Members of the congregation use
Love to Pray to deepen and strengthen their personal prayer lives. At
the same time the church plans sermons, small group opportunities,
prayer training for children and teens, and prayer activities around the
themes of *Love to Pray*. After the *40 Days of Prayer* the church continues
on with prayer ministries that build on the prayer foundations that have
been laid.

The following resources are available for churches planning to initiate
40 Days of Prayer:

◆ **40 Days of Prayer Strategy Guidelines**—A comprehensive resource
  for planning and implementing *40 Days of Prayer*.
◆ **Love to Pray**—A devotional book on prayer with group study guide.
  All members of the churches are encouraged to use this book.
◆ **Love to Pray DVD**—Prayer leaders introduce each of the *Love to
  Pray* group study sessions with a 15-minute presentation.
◆ **Sermons on Prayer**—Biblically based sermon outlines correspond
  to *Love to Pray* themes.
◆ **Additional Resources**—A CD with *40 Days of Prayer* graphics and
  sample segments of the teaching video; a prayer course for teens:
  Can I Call after Midnight?; and a prayer course for children: *Kids
  Love to Pray Too*.

Scripture makes prayer the priority of the church. The early church
was devoted to prayer (Acts 2:42). Its leaders were devoted to prayer (Acts
6:4). The Holy Spirit stresses devotion to prayer (Col. 4:2) and commands
believers to, "Pray in the Spirit on all occasions with all kinds of prayers
and requests . . . and always keep on praying for all the saints" (Eph. 6:18).
Prayer is meant to be at the very heart and soul of every church's life.

Dr. Paul Cedar, one of the presenters on the DVD in the *Love to Pray*
group study course, has said, "Prayer is life's greatest joy, highest privilege, and most powerful venture. Nothing can compare to it." If that is
true—and my experience tells me it is—then deepening your personal

prayer life will give you a tremendous spiritual lift. And lifting the prayer life and developing the prayer ministries of your local church will yield wonderful results.

I urge you to press on in the journey of learning to *love to pray*. God is inviting you to do great things and prayer is at the heart of it.

—*Alvin J. VanderGriend*

Resources available from:

40daysofprayer.net
PrayerShop Publishing: 1-800-217-5200

Preface

This book is a by-product of my personal prayer journey. It's a journey that led to a better understanding of prayer, greater intimacy with God, and eventually to *loving to pray*—at least most of the time.

I was taught to pray from childhood. The first prayer I remember was the mealtime prayer "Lord, bless this food and drink, for Jesus' sake. Amen." My parents encouraged me to pray when I got up in the morning and when I went to bed at night. They led us in prayer before and after each meal.

But there was a lot about prayer I didn't know. I didn't know prayer was all about relationship—a love relationship with the Father. I didn't know that I had to ask for spiritual blessings in order to receive them. I didn't know what a difference intercession could make. Learned phrases made up much of my prayers. "Forgive us our many sins" at the end of a prayer sufficed for confession. "Gracious heavenly Father," a standard prayer-starter, covered praise. A habitual "in Jesus' name" wrapped things up before the "Amen" ending.

Prayer was mostly a way to keep in touch with God, something you did upon rising, over meals, and at bedtime. You could do it all with familiar phrases and in about five minutes a day.

I am deeply grateful for what I *did* learn about prayer through my Christian upbringing. Some important foundations *were* laid. But as I tried to grow in my prayer life in later years, I always got stuck. Every new effort—and there were many—ended in failure. I didn't even like to pray. The major problem was, I discovered, that I didn't really understand what prayer was—not at its heart.

My understanding of prayer came little by little. First, I learned that if I asked "in accord with God's will," he would give me "whatever I asked." I came to understand that prayer was a way to experience intimacy with God. Then came further insights: intercession is a way to partner with God, serious confession restores a love relationship, and extended times of praise are pure joy. Prayer, I came to see, was key to true spirituality.

This booklet is written for persons who want to *learn to love to pray*. I want to assure you that it is possible to learn to love to pray. You see loving to pray is really about loving the One to whom we pray. And we who know and love the Lord can all do that.

May God bless you richly as you embark on this adventure of learning to love to pray.

Prayerfully yours, in Christ,
Alvin J. Vander Griend

Contents

WEEK ONE

WHAT'S THE GOOD OF PRAYER?

Day One

Friendship with God

You have made known to me the path of life;
you will fill me with joy in your presence,
with eternal pleasures at your right hand.
PSALM 16:11

Human beings are created to live in fellowship with God. We are meant to have and to enjoy life in relationship with God. Without this relationship we are like branches cut off from a tree, like toasters not plugged in.

Prayer is the way we get in touch with God and the way we keep in touch with him. I used to think of prayer as a spiritual exercise, a discipline that had to be worked at. Through the years, however, God has taught me to see it more and more as the talking part of a friendship. One of the early church fathers called it "keeping company with God." I like that!

Several years ago as I tried to define prayer, God led me through a series of steps. At first I thought of prayer simply as *talking with God*. Then, the idea of relationship emerged, and I began to see that prayer is the talking part of a *relationship* with God. Months later my definition changed again, and I began to understand that prayer is the talking part of a love relationship with God. But there was still more I had to learn. I came to see that prayer was the talking part of the *most important* love relationship in our lives. With that addition I thought that I finally had it, but some years later God added one more element. Then the definition, a definition that I still live with today, came out as: "prayer is the conversational part of the most important love relationship in our lives, *our love relationship with the Father, the Son and the Holy Spirit*".

Sometimes people ask how much time they should try to spend in prayer each day. I used to suggest that 20 minutes of formal prayer a day was a minimum. I reinforced that by reminding them of the many things that need to be included in a prayer, and then I added that 20 minutes a day was only about 2 percent of our waking hours each day.

Now when people ask about the time they should spend in prayer, I simply tell them they should spend enough time to build a good relationship. And, considering that the relationship we are talking about is life's most important love relationship, that means plenty of time.

What does God do for those who relate to him in love? The psalmist put it well when he said, "You will fill me with joy in your presence, with eternal pleasures at your right hand."

What's the good of prayer? Just this! It helps us to grow into and live out of that most important of all love relationships. But, of course, it's only as good as we make it. So, what good are you making of it?

Reflect

♦ What can your prayer life tell you about your love relationship with God?

♦ What more could you do to deepen your friendship with God?

Pray

♦ *Praise* God for his love and for his readiness to have a love relationship with you.

♦ *Ask* God to strengthen your prayer life and deepen your relationship with him.

♦ *Ask* God to fill you with joy in his presence and to give you eternal pleasures at his right hand.

♦ *Thank* God for his generosity in making these gifts available.

Act

Intentionally set aside some time to spend with God. Do some relationship-building things with him during that time. Write down the three most important things that you got out of your time with God.

✵

Day Two

Prayer Starts with God

*²⁶The Spirit helps us in our weakness. We do not know what we
ought to pray for, but the Spirit himself intercedes for us with
groans that words cannot express. ²⁷And he who searches our
hearts knows the mind of the Spirit, because the Spirit intercedes
for the saints in accord with God's will.*
ROMANS 8:26-27

I want to share a radical thought. It has transformed my way of praying
and my way of thinking about prayer.

For years I believed that my prayers started with me. I had to think
them up. I had to get God's attention. Not surprisingly, with this frame of
mind, prayer was often a chore.

I learned that I was wrong. Prayer doesn't start with us. *Prayer starts
with God.* That's the radical idea that changed my prayer life. God is the
initiator. He moves us to pray. He gives us prayer ideas. He holds out the
promises we claim in prayer. When we pray, we are God's instruments.

God is at work in all our praying. He makes his will known to us so
that we will ask for the very things he longs to give us. Out of love he
burdens us to pray for others so that, in response to our intercession, he
can pour out blessings on them.

And it's the Spirit, says Paul, that makes our prayer possible. We don't
know what to pray, but we don't have to. The Spirit is there revealing
God's will to us in the Scriptures and bringing God's prayer concerns
to life within us. He is nudging us through circumstances and opening
our eyes to the needs around us. He is searching our hearts and trying
our ways so that he can bring us to true repentance. He is revealing the
glory and the goodness of God so that our prayers will be filled with
praise and thanks.

We can be confident that God will hear when we come to him. God answers every prayer that starts in heaven, every prayer born in our hearts by the Holy Spirit, every prayer based on a sure promise from his Word.

If prayer starts with God, then the first order of business as we learn to pray is to learn to listen to God's whispers, to tune our hearts to him, to respond to his promptings. Perhaps the first prayer of each day should be "Lord, teach me to pray. Help me to understand your purposes, to feel your burdens, to see what you see, to hear the groans you hear, so that my prayers may be pleasing to you and may accomplish your purposes."

How about starting right now: "Lord, teach me to pray today."

Reflect
- Is prayer a chore or a joy for you?
- What more could you do to be sure that you truly know God's will when you pray?

Pray
- *Praise* the Lord as the prayer-initiating, prayer-hearing God.
- *Ask* God to make prayer a joy in your life.
- *Thank* God for the privilege of knowing his thoughts and praying them back to him.
- *Intercede* for loved ones who may be weak in prayer.

Act
The next time you set aside time to pray, start by saying, "Lord, help me right now to know what you want me to pray." Be open to praise, thanks, confession or supplication. Wait for impressions or promptings from the Spirit. When they come, pray them.

✳

Day Three

Celebrating God Through Prayer

¹I will extol the Lord at all times;
his praise will always be on my lips.
²My soul boasts in the Lord;
let the afflicted hear and rejoice.
³Glorify the Lord with me;
let us exalt his name together.
PSALM 34:1-3

Everyone loves a good celebration. And life gives us plenty of opportunities to celebrate. We celebrate Christmas, the new year, birthdays,
anniversaries, graduations, victories, and more. But there is no better reason to celebrate than God.

To celebrate means "to honor or praise publicly." God deserves hon-
or and praise more than anyone or anything else. The great Scottish
preacher Alexander Whyte used to counsel his hearers to "think magnificently of God." People who think magnificently of God, calling to
mind his greatness and goodness, cannot help but celebrate God and
declare his praise.

We live in a society that delights to celebrate worth. We exalt Super
Bowl heroes, we gush over favorite movie stars, and we glory in our
nations' victories. Not all of that is bad. But in the process of lifting up and
extolling let's not forget the One who is the source of all good things.

To celebrate God means at least three things:

First, it means *recognizing God for who he is*. God's glory is his majestic
splendor shining out so it can be seen and known. When we glorify God,

we don't give him anything. We don't add luster to him. That's as impossible as it is to add splendor to a sunset by viewing it. But we can gaze in wonder at a sunset, and similarly we can behold in awe the beauty and glory of the Lord.

Second, it means *loving God for who he is.* This means laying aside our concerns, our demands, and our prayer lists to focus on God and to enjoy him. Nothing does more to quell pride, self-centeredness, and selfish desires than to focus beyond ourselves on God alone.

Third, celebrating God means *giving God the only thing we can offer him*—our loving, praising hearts. He already has everything else. He is totally self-sufficient and needs nothing from us. But God does ask us to give to him our hearts, our love, and our adoration. When we do, he is pleased and blessed.

Let's start today by thinking "magnificently of God." Everything else will follow.

Reflect

◆ How much do you enjoy God? Do you ever take personal time just to think about God and his goodness and to worship him?

◆ Think of some specific ways that you can celebrate God today.

Pray

◆ *Praise* God by telling him five things you especially appreciate about him.

◆ *Ask* God to help you see his majestic splendor and to truly enjoy him and love him.

◆ *Thank* God for revealing his glory and for giving you reason to boast about him.

◆ *Confess*, if there has been little heartfelt praise for God in your life, and ask his forgiveness.

Act

Set aside some time today to gaze on God. That may mean letting your mind dwell on several of God's attributes—his love, his wisdom, his power, and his grace. Reflect your thoughts and feelings back to God. (See Appendix C for a "Prayers of Praise" experience.)

✳

Day Four

Does God Need Our Prayers?

> *⁹Moses said to Joshua, "Choose some of our men and go out to*
> *fight the Amalekites. . . . I will stand on top of the hill with*
> *the staff of God in my hands." . . .*
> *¹¹As long as Moses held up his hands, the Israelites were*
> *winning, but whenever he lowered his hands,*
> *the Amalekites were winning.*
> EXODUS 17:9, 11
> (FOR THE FULL STORY, READ EXODUS 17:8-16.)

God sometimes teaches us in surprising ways. When Israel faced a serious military threat, Joshua and the army went out to fight, but Moses went up on a hillside to pray. When his praying hands were up, Israel was winning. But when they were down, the enemy was winning.

Why, we may ask, would God allow his people to suffer defeat when there was no prayer? The answer is that God was teaching his people that he chooses to move in response to prayer and that he will not move without it.

Though he is almighty, all-wise, and fully able to work without us, God chooses to work through our prayers. He calls us into a working partnership. We co-labor with him to accomplish his purposes. Things happen when we pray that won't happen if we don't pray.

When God first taught me this important principle of prayer, it had a simple but pointed application for me. It was as if God said, "Alvin, when your children go to school each morning, they are heading into battle. If you as a parent keep your hands uplifted, they will be winning. But, if your praying hands come down, they will be losing." I have never forgotten that lesson.

Since that time I have come to see that as church leaders and faithful Christians "lift up holy hands in prayer" (1 Timothy 2:8), the church grows strong and is able to break down the gates of hell. When believers in neighborhoods and workplaces lift up praying hands over those around them, the powers of darkness are pushed back.

The most common testimony of *Lighthouse** keepers as they pray over neighborhoods is that of transformation. They speak of crack houses closing, crime rates falling, marriages being restored, families coming back together, and people being converted. What's happening as God's people pray over their neighborhoods is the same thing that happened as Moses prayed over the battlefield. The forces of evil go into retreat.

What we need most for solving the problems in our society is not more money, more education, more ideas, books, or strategies. Our prime need is hands lifted up in prayer. "We can accomplish far more by our prayers than by our work. Prayer . . . can do anything God can do! When we pray, God works" (*The Kneeling Christian*). Where are your hands right now?

Reflect

♦ Where in God's kingdom are people winning against the powers of darkness because of your prayers? Are there places where they appear to be losing because there is little prayer?

♦ What kinds of things do you think God might want to do on your street or at your workplace in response to your prayers?

Pray

♦ Praise God for the wisdom of his plan to govern the world through the prayers of his people.

♦ Ask God to help you understand why your prayers are so important to him.

♦ Thank God for honoring you by choosing to act in response to your prayers.

♦ Commit yourself to pray faithfully for family members, neighbors, or coworkers so that God may work in response to your prayers.

Act

Stand outside your home or apartment. Look around. What is the evil one attempting to do in the lives of those who live near you? Lift your hands in prayer over this neighborhood (or at least visualize yourself doing it). Imagine God, in response to your prayers, moving to frustrate what the devil is trying to do.

* A Lighthouse, as referred to in this devotional, is a person, family, or small group that commits to praying for, caring for, and sharing the gospel of Jesus Christ with their neighbors, co-workers, friends, or family members.

WEEK ONE

❁

Day Five

Your Welcome to the Throne

Let us then approach the throne of grace with confidence,
so that we may receive mercy and find grace to help us
in our time of need.
HEBREWS 4:16

Access to the throne of God is the foundation of all prayer. All prayers must approach the throne. Every true believer is welcome there.

Access to God's throne is an amazing privilege. The One we approach is the sovereign, all-powerful, holy Ruler of the universe. What a privilege to be welcomed into his presence!

God's throne, we are reminded, is a throne of grace, not a throne of judgment. This means that if we have come into his presence through the blood of Christ, we are acceptable to him. God doesn't scrutinize us to screen out unworthiness. He extends a hand of welcome.

We are invited to approach with complete confidence. We won't run into a closed door. We won't have to beg or grovel to get in. God is expecting us. He is glad we have come.

Sometimes when I pray, I like to imagine myself right there in the throne room of heaven. In my mind's eye I see the One upon the throne high and lifted up. His glory fills the room. I see angels all around. It's enough to overpower me with dread, except for one thing: God recognizes me. He knows my name. He looks at me, smiles, and extends a hand of welcome. "Tell me why you have come," he says.

This wonderful welcome is extended to us not because we are so good and worthy in ourselves. The truth is, we deserve to be barred from God's presence because of our sins. But Christ has dealt with our sins and made us acceptable to God. We have been adopted as sons and daughters. We have a place in the royal family.

We can come to the throne with our own concerns. We can also come, as intercessors, with the needs of our families, friends, and neighbors on our hearts.

Lighthouse intercessors regularly talk to God on behalf of their neighbors. One *Lighthouse* keeper reported that after she and others had prayed for their neighbors for about a year, neighbors became more friendly, people stopped abusing drugs, two unemployed women found jobs, a father stopped drinking, a woman was miraculously cured, a person was delivered from an evil spirit, several persons came to know Christ, and a Bible study began. Wow! What was happening in the throne room had a transforming effect on earth.

That's something of what God has in mind by extending his welcome to us. He wants to change us, and he wants to change our world.

Reflect
- How much confidence do you have when you pray?
- Try to think of at least three reasons why it is possible for believers to approach the throne of God with confidence.
- Think of some ways that you can increase your confidence.

Pray
- *Praise* God for making his grace and mercy available for the asking.
- *Thank* God that he welcomes you into his throne room.
- *Ask* God for the mercy and grace he generously offers you, and for the confidence you need so that you can pray effectively for yourself and others.

Act
Take a prayerwalk around your neighborhood. Prayerwalking is "praying on-site with insight." Let what you see inform your prayers.

WEEK TWO

THE REQUIREMENTS OF PRAYER

✹

Day One

The Necessity of a Clean Heart

18If I had cherished sin in my heart,
the Lord would not have listened;
19but God has surely listened
and heard my voice in prayer.
PSALM 66:18-19

Sin hinders prayer. A person may pray and pray without receiving an answer, and then conclude that the problem is in God. In reality the problem may be in the person's heart. David understood that if he cherished sin in his heart, the Lord would not hear him.

One of the worst things about sin is that it obstructs prayer. We are shut out from God when we cherish sin because God is holy and cannot tolerate sin in his presence.

When sin blocks prayer, the real problem is not that we have sinned but that, having sinned, we have not repented. It is only unconfessed sin, cherished in our hearts, that inhibits our prayers. Forgiven sin does not hinder prayer. Forgiven sinners are welcome in God's presence.

Always eager to have us come into his presence, God has provided a way for sin to be removed through Jesus' blood so that we can come and not be hindered. John says, "If we confess our sins, he is faithful and just and will forgive us our sins and purify us from all unrighteousness" (1 John 1:9). When it's forgiven, our sin is gone, and it no longer impedes.

The first requirement of prayer, then, is to confess anything in your heart that is not of God. When your sin is forgiven, you can be confident that God will hear and answer your prayers.

Don't be afraid to take inventory and to deal with what you find. Recently when I was confronted with a list of twenty sin-identifying Scripture texts, I at first thought, "My heart is clean before God. I don't have anything to confess." But I went through the list anyway, and to my amazement I found five areas of sin that needed to be dealt with. So I clearly identified what was offensive to God, confessed those things, and claimed God's forgiving grace. Through that I again discovered complete freedom in prayer. We can't have the privilege of prayer without purity of heart.

Not only does sin hinder prayer; prayer hinders sin. The two are always opposed. The more careless we are about sin, the less we will pray. The more we pray, the less careless we will be about sin. Both sin and prayer are powerful forces. Which one is moving you?

Reflect

◆ Is there any area of your life about which you are uneasy before God? Risk taking a closer look at it. You may find a "cherished" sin.

◆ Can you say to yourself with confidence what David said: "God has surely listened and heard my voice in prayer"?

Pray

◆ *Praise* God that "he is faithful and just and will forgive us our sins" (1 John 1:9).

◆ *Ask* God to search your heart and life and to reveal to you any sin you may need to deal with.

◆ *Confess* any sin that the Spirit brings to your attention.

◆ *Thank* God for forgiving your sin and purifying you from all unrighteousness so that you can go confidently into his presence.

Act

Read the list of do's and don'ts in Romans 12:9-21. Put a checkmark by any one of these commands that you are failing to keep. Say a prayer of confession for specific sins you may discover in this way. Ask the Lord to clear your record and cleanse your heart. Make a fresh commitment.

✳

Day Two

The Faith That Receives

22"Have faith in God," Jesus answered . . . . 24"Therefore I tell you, whatever you ask for in prayer, believe that you have received it, and it will be yours."
MARK 11:22-24

Faith is a second requirement of true prayer. Prayers without faith are incomplete. Millions of prayers have been prayed with no faith and have thus failed in their intent. They have not been true prayers.

The astounding promise Jesus makes in Mark 11:24 seems to offer too much. How can God offer to do "whatever [we] ask for in prayer"? And why have so many believers asked, trusting God, and not received?

The difficulty we have with this passage is really a difficulty in understanding faith. We tend to think of faith as a personal possession that exists wholly within us. We figure that if we have enough faith, we'll get what we ask for—and if we don't, we won't get it.

But faith is not simply a possession. It's an aspect of relationship. It's not something we own like an idea or a feeling. Faith always involves another person. It trusts the other person to think and act in a certain way. For example, throughout all the years my parents were alive, I knew they would welcome me anytime I came home. I knew they loved me. I trusted that they cared for me and were willing to help me anytime. In other words, I had faith in them. This faith was based on what I knew about them. Faith in God is like that. It's a conviction about who God is, what he is like, and how he will always act.

Praying in faith is not an inner conviction that God will act according to our desires if only we believe hard enough. It involves believing that God will always respond to our prayers in accord with his nature, his purposes, and his promises.

God does not want us simply to toss requests at him, hoping that some of them will be answered. He wants us to ask, knowing he is there, claiming what he promises, trusting that he will act in line with his nature and that his purposes will be achieved. That's praying in faith.

When you ask a person for something in good faith, you don't ask for something the person would not be willing to give. I could never, for example, ask my parents to give me more than my share of their inheritance. I know them too well to make such a selfish and unfair request. Similarly, if you truly know God, you will only ask for what is in accord with his will and not for anything that is purely selfish.

If you want to grow strong in prayer, grow strong in faith. If you want to grow strong in faith, get to know God better. If you want to get to know God better, spend time with him, reading his Word and listening to his Spirit.

Reflect

♦ Why do you think God has made faith such an indispensable condition of prayer?
♦ What kinds of things can you do to increase your faith?

Pray

♦ *Praise* God for being trustworthy.
♦ *Ask* God to increase your faith so that you can pray more powerfully.
♦ *Thank* God for his willingness to hear and answer the prayers you bring to him in faith.
♦ *Confess* any lack of faith you may discover in yourself.

Act

Try this prayer of faith experiment. Read James 1:5 and note that it reveals both the nature of God and a promise of God. If you are *sure* of God's nature as revealed in this verse and *sure* that God will deliver on his promise, ask for wisdom in connection with some practical issue you are facing right now. Believe without doubt that God will supply it. Thank him in advance for the wisdom he will provide. Keep asking and trusting until you receive the wisdom you asked for.

✳

Day Three

The Life That Can Pray

*²¹We have confidence before God ²²and receive from him
anything we ask, because we obey his commands and
do what pleases him.*
1 JOHN 3:21-22

Obedience is fundamental to effective prayer. Only people who obey
God have the right to go into his presence with requests.

God delights in the prayers of his obedient children. When we want
what God wants and live the way he likes, then we will tend to pray
prayers that God will answer in the way we expect. And God, in answering our prayers, is supporting what he approves. Were God to answer the
prayers of the disobedient, he would be aiding and abetting what he does
not approve. That would be out of character for God.

To put it in other words, if we expect God to do for us what we ask, we
should be prepared to do for God what he asks. If we listen to his words
of command, God will listen to our words of request.

This principle also explains much of the weakness of prayer. Lack of
power, lack of perseverance, and lack of confidence in prayer all stem
from some lack in the Christian life. Often when prayer fails and we
receive no answers, we assume the problem is in God while in reality the
problem really is in us.

The obedience God expects of us is not beyond our reach. God, who
is committed to hearing the prayers of his obedient children, also gives
enabling grace so that we are able to live obediently. Touched by his grace
and with his Spirit living in us, we have both the desire and the strength
to do God's will.

If you want to become powerful in prayer, spend time with the Lord
and spend time in the Word. That's where you will find the will of God

clearly stated. Let "the word of Christ dwell in you richly" and control what you do and say (Colossians 3:16). Jesus reminds us that if we remain in him, and his words remain in us, we may ask whatever we wish and it will be given us (John 15:7).

Or, to put it more simply, let me ask, Do you want to have confidence when you pray and receive from God what you ask for? Then begin by living a life of obedience. That's the bottom line.

Reflect

♦ What difference do you think confidence will make in your prayer life?

♦ What kinds of things will confident pray-ers ask for?

♦ What kinds of things do you think God is eager to give to those who obey his commands?

Pray

♦ *Praise* God for his generous, giving nature.

♦ *Confess* any failure to keep God's commands or to do what pleases him—sins that may be keeping you from effective prayer.

♦ *Ask* God for the desires of your obedient heart. Expect him to give what you ask.

♦ *Thank* God for this amazing promise to answer your prayers.

Act

Pray for yourself Paul's prayer from Colossians 1:9-12—a prayer that he prayed for the Colossian Christians. As God answers, you will be growing spiritually in a way that will provide underpinnings of obedience for your prayer life.

WEEK TWO

❋

Day Four

Praying in Jesus' Name

"Until now you have not asked for anything in my name. Ask
and you will receive, and your joy will be complete."
JOHN 16:24

By offering to let us pray in his name, Jesus is offering an amazingly great privilege. It's as if he is giving us blank checks to be drawn on his account, knowing we will use them for his honor and his advantage. Jesus is demonstrating great trust in us. He is trusting that his honor and his interests are safe in our hands. Consider what it would mean to place your estate in the hands of another person: your credit cards, your home, your investments, your automobiles, your responsibilities, everything. You'd pick that person very carefully, wouldn't you? You'd really be giving that person control over your life and your future.

That's essentially what Jesus did when he authorized us to use his name in prayer. He gave us authority over his accounts. He asked us to exercise control over his estate—the kingdom of God.

We exercise our authority by prayer. By prayer we ask the Father for all we need in order to do the job. By prayer we ask God to deal with demonic forces contrary to his will. By prayer we direct God's grace and power to strategic locations where it is needed.

Three phrases in particular help us understand what it means to pray in Jesus' name. First, we are *authorized to be Christ's representatives.* When we come to the Father in Jesus' name, we come as those who are authorized to act in his place. We "represent" him. When we stand before the throne, the Father recognizes us as persons who stand in the place of his Son. That makes us acceptable.

Second, we come to God *on the basis of Christ's merit.* You and I have no claim on God, but Christ does. He merited the Father's favor by his perfect life and sacrifice. When we come in Jesus' name, we are identified with him. We come on the ground of his claim on the Father. Our access depends solely on what Jesus has done.

Try to imagine yourself coming to the Father on your own, apart from Christ. You are unauthorized to come, because you have no claim on God's favor. In fact, you have a huge debt with God because of your sins and you can expect nothing but God's blazing wrath. That's the opposite of coming in the name of Jesus.

Third, we come asking *in accord with Christ's will*. We have the mind of Christ in us, so what we ask is what Jesus would ask. He is asking us to ask for him. We are able to ask what he would ask because our wills are in sync with his will.

The Father so loves the Son that when we introduce the Son's name in prayer, we have his ear, we have secured his willingness, and we have touched his heart.

Reflect

 ◆ Think about the responsibility you have for building some part of Christ's kingdom. What help do you need from the Lord to do this well?
 ◆ What can you do to learn how to be more conscious of Jesus' will as you pray in his name?
 ◆ Have you ever added the words "in Jesus name" to a prayer when, in fact, the prayer did not really represent his will?

Pray

 ◆ *Praise* God for the gracious provision of his Son, Jesus Christ, as the One through whom you are able to approach the throne and receive a hearing from God.
 ◆ *Confess* any selfish praying that has not truly represented the mind of Christ and has not been in accord with his will.
 ◆ *Ask* for anything you need in order to accomplish God's will in your life and in your world.

Act

Instead of ending your prayers "in Jesus name," try using an expanded version of this phrase, like "I am asking this, Lord, because your Son authorized me to do so and because I am certain it is what he wants me to ask. Grant it, not because of any worth in me, but because your Son has earned it."

✳

Day Five

Praying With Persistence

*Jesus told his disciples a parable to show them that they
should always pray and not give up.*
LUKE 18:1
(READ LUKE 18:1-8 FOR THE SETTING OF JESUS' PARABLE.)

Prayer is not always easy. Sometimes it requires serious persistence in the face of great difficulty and delayed answers. God wants us to rise above weakness and become mighty in prayer. The parable of the persistent widow in Luke 18:2-8 strikingly illustrates this principle.

To pray persistently is to press our requests upon God with urgency and perseverance. It means praying boldly and with determination until the answer comes.

When God delays his answers to prayer, it is always with good reason. Sometimes he does it to deepen our faith and develop our character. Sometimes he does it to test our faith and put it on display. Sometimes he is simply operating according to a divine timetable that seems slow to us. When answers seem slow in coming, it's important to keep trusting and keep asking.

God has called us to persistent prayer so that his will may be done on earth and his name may be glorified. We may never use prayer for selfish reasons. Prayer is the means by which God accomplishes his purposes and defeats Satan. Through prayer we are involved with God in a grand enterprise. And the going is not always easy.

George Mueller is a good example of persistence in prayer. He prayed daily for five unsaved friends. One of them came to Christ after five years; two more were converted after fifteen years. The fourth was saved after thirty-five years of prayer, and the fifth became a child of God just after Mueller's death.

Passion in prayer is usually tied closely to perseverance in prayer. Passion does not spring simply from human emotion or earnestness of soul. It's an urgency derived from God who, through his Spirit within us, gives us both the content and the passion of our prayers.

Weak and feeble praying does not have the power to overcome difficulties and gain the victory. E. M. Bounds asserted, "Heaven pays little attention to casual requests. God is not moved by feeble desires, listless prayers, and spiritual laziness."

There is great need today for powerful, persistent prayer. Much is accomplished through persistent prayer that is not accomplished by timid, halting prayers. God has much to accomplish through you—in your world, in your church, in your family, and in your neighborhood. I urge you to partner with God through passionate, persistent prayer.

Reflect

+ Which comes closer to describing your intercessory prayer life: bold, passionate, and persevering or casual, weak, and fainthearted?
+ What things in your life do you think God wants you to pray about persistently?

Pray

+ *Praise* God, who hears prayer and "brings about justice for his chosen ones, who cry to him day and night" (Luke 18:7).
+ *Confess* whatever casualness, weakness, feebleness, superficiality, laxity, faintheartedness, or impatience you may discover as you examine your prayer life.
+ *Ask* the Holy Spirit for boldness, power, devotion, persistence, and a sense of urgency in your prayer life.
+ *Thank* God for the privilege of partnering with him through prayer in accomplishing his will on earth.

Act

Is there something that you used to pray for, something you *know* God wants to see happen (like the conversion of a loved one), that you have stopped praying for? If so, start praying again, and be persistent. Try to imagine as you pray that each prayer brings the matter a little closer to the answer.

WEEK THREE

CLAIMING GOD'S RICHES

✻

Day One

Asking For Ourselves

Let us then approach the throne of grace with confidence,
so that we may receive mercy and find grace to help us
in our time of need.
HEBREWS 4:16 (ALSO READ VV. 14-15)

"Whether we like it or not," said Charles H. Spurgeon, "asking is the rule of the kingdom." God delights in our asking because we are his children. His Father-heart leaps for joy when we come asking. This kind of prayer keeps drawing us back into the dependency of the parent-child relationship.

Petition is asking God for our personal needs. I want to emphasize here that it's okay to request God's blessings for ourselves. Some people think petition (asking for ourselves) is a more primitive form of prayer, reflecting a still-somewhat-selfish spirituality, while prayers of praise, thanksgiving, and intercession reflect a higher kind of spirituality.

That's unbiblical thinking. We are forever dependent on God, so we need constantly to be asking for his blessing on us. God has much to give, and we have great need. Petitionary prayer connects our needs to God's generosity. The Bible is full of it.

Jesus unabashedly commends petitionary prayer. To encourage his disciples in prayer, he said, "I say to you: Ask and it will be given to you; seek and you will find; knock and the door will be opened to you. For everyone who asks receives; he who seeks finds; and to him who knocks, the door will be opened" (Luke 11:9-10). God likes to have his children ask. He is not bothered by our asking, even when we come to him with the smallest details of our lives.

In Hebrews 4:16 we are urged to approach God's throne of grace with confidence to receive what we need from him. God invites us to come with confidence in the awareness that Jesus has opened the way to God's Father-heart for our sake and that he is committed to meeting our needs. And we are able to come with confidence that Jesus will understand, for he "has been tempted in every way, just as we are—yet was without sin" (Hebrews 4:15).

The Lord invites us to come with a consciousness of our sin, asking for mercy—not to receive the punishment we really deserve. He invites us to come with a consciousness of our needs, asking for grace—that we receive what we do not deserve. Jesus stands ready to meet us, no matter what our need may be.

It's an insult to God not to come asking. Saint Theresa of Avila once declared, "You pay God a compliment by asking great things of him." What are you going to ask?

Reflect

- Have you ever felt complimented by being asked for help? Why might asking be a way to compliment God? Why might God be insulted if we don't ask?
- Why do you suppose that God, knowing us better than we know ourselves, has invited us to come asking?

Pray

- *Praise* Jesus Christ, our heavenly High Priest, who has entered into the heavenly throne room for us, who is also able to sympathize fully with us.
- If you have failed to regularly approach the throne of grace to ask for mercy and grace, *confess* this as an insult to God and a failure to recognize the true nature of your dependence on him.
- *Thank* God for his readiness to forgive and to help you in your need.
- *Approach* God with confidence and *ask* for the mercy he has promised and for the grace to help you with any specific need.

Act

Make a list of at least three good things that you know your loving, heavenly Father really wants you to have (things like joy, self-control, brotherly kindness), and persistently ask for them with complete confidence that God is pleased with your asking and is most eager to help.

✸

Day Two

Asking For Good Things

> [9]"Which of you, if his son asks for bread, will give him a stone?
> [10]Or if he asks for a fish, will give him a snake? [11]If you, then,
> though you are evil, know how to give good gifts to your children,
> how much more will your Father in heaven give good gifts
> to those who ask him!"
> MATTHEW 7:9-11

As a father, I have always wanted good things for our four children. I have deeply desired that they have firm faith, wholesome morals, excellent educational opportunities, fine friends, good jobs, strong marriages, lovely children, and stable lives. I have hoped and prayed that their lives may be full of love, joy, and peace. I have wanted all this despite the fact that, as an earthly father, I don't hold a candle to the heavenly Father.

Jesus makes clear that our heavenly Father, who is perfect in his love and unlimited in power, wants good things for us, his children. And he assures us that the Father is willing to give good gifts to his children, much more willing than any earthly father or mother.

There's just one hitch. In order to receive the good things the Father wants for them, his children have to ask. Not to ask is not to receive. That's what some spiritually deprived believers found out the hard way. James said them, "You do not have, because you do not ask God" (James 4:2).

The "good gifts" Jesus has in mind are the spiritual blessings of grace, wisdom, joy, peace, power, holiness, and so on. These are things in accord with God's will. We can ask the Father for them with absolute assurance that he will give them to us. It's what he has promised.

What an amazing promise! Getting hold of this promise revolutionized my spiritual life. I searched the Scriptures for the good things God wanted for me. I asked for them. And, true to his promise, God began to give them—not in huge once-for-all doses, but little by little. Every time I began to ask for some new good thing, if I watched closely, I began to see God working that good thing into my life.

God is eager to give. He's on the lookout for children who will take him at his word and ask in faith. As one Old Testament prophet put it, "The eyes of the Lord range throughout the earth to strengthen those whose hearts are fully committed to him" (2 Chronicles 16:9).

God is probably looking at you right now and waiting for you to ask good things of him. I have a feeling he'll be disappointed if you don't go for the max and ask him for all sorts of really good things—things that he is really eager to give you—right now.

Reflect
+ What good things would you give to your family members or friends if you could?
+ What do you prize most highly among God's good gifts?
+ Why is it important to God that we ask?

Pray
+ *Praise* the Father, who in his power and love is able and willing to give "good gifts" to those who ask.
+ *Confess* any attempt to fill your life with worldly things instead of the good things the Father wants to give you.
+ *Ask* for all the spiritually good things you can think of.
+ *Thank* God in advance for what he will send in response to your prayer.

Act
Continue to ask for the good things you prayed for yesterday. (It's a good idea to make a list so that you can remember them.) Pray those requests again today, trying to think of all the reasons why your heavenly Father would want to give them to you. Can you think of any reason he wouldn't want to give them?

WEEK THREE

❋

Day Three

Getting What We Ask For

*¹⁴This is the confidence we have in approaching God: that if we
ask anything according to his will, he hears us. ¹⁵And if we know
that he hears us—whatever we ask—we know that we
have what we asked of him.*

1 JOHN 5:14-15

Imagine what it would be like to approach God in prayer and to receive
from him anything and everything we asked for. I'm sure we would do
a lot of asking if that were the case. Once the pattern of asking and receiving was established, we'd be bold to go back and ask for more.

Well, God doesn't promise to give us anything and everything we
ask for. But he does make an astonishing promise to pray-ers that is
even better. He promises to give us whatever we ask that is "according
to his will."

To ask for what is according to God's will is to ask for the very things
God wants for us. These are the things he knows we need, the things that
are truly good for us, the riches of his grace that he wants us to have.

How do we know what is according to God's will? We look in the Bible.
There God tells us what he most wants for us.

When I first understood this principle and wanted to pray in accord
with God's will, the Holy Spirit took me to Romans 8:29 and reminded me
that God wanted me "to be conformed to the likeness of his Son." Then I
did a very simple thing. I said, "God, please conform me to the image of
your Son." That was the first prayer I consciously prayed in accord with
God's will. God heard me and began in me the process that answered that
prayer. He's still working at it today.

After that, I found many things to ask for that were in line with God's
will for me. I asked for wisdom, faith, virtue, love, joy, godliness, prayerful-

40

ness, Spirit-filledness, and much more. I know God heard those prayers. I began to see the difference it made in me. What I usually observed was a definite but gradual change in the right direction.

If you want to grow spiritually and to claim the riches God has for you, simply ask for those things in accord with God's will. He will hear, and you will receive what you ask of him. God has promised to give what you ask for in accord with his will.

And if what you ask for happens to be outside of God's will and you don't receive it, thank God! What's outside of his will isn't good for you anyway.

Reflect

- ◆ Think about the patterns you practice in prayer. Are you used to approaching God with confidence that he will hear and respond, or do you pray just hoping something will happen?
- ◆ What things can you ask God for right now that you know are in line with his will for you?
- ◆ Are you so confident that you "know that [you] have" what you have asked of God and are watching for the answer?

Pray

- ◆ *Praise* God for the wisdom by which he knows what is best for you, and for the power to do what he promises.
- ◆ *Confess* if you find that because of weakness in your prayers you have failed to claim the riches God has promised you.
- ◆ *Ask* God for spiritual riches that you know are "according to his will" for your life.
- ◆ *Thank* God for what he will give even before you actually receive it. If you can honestly do this, it's a sure sign that you really trust God to deliver on his promise.

Act

Add to your petitionary prayers—if you haven't done so already—the most important things that you think God wants to give you. Be ready to pray for those things long-term. (See Appendix F for the authors helpful A-Z petitionary prayer list.)

Day Four

The Cure For Anxiety

*⁶Do not be anxious about anything, but in everything, by prayer
and petition, with thanksgiving, present your requests to God.
⁷And the peace of God, which transcends all understanding, will
guard your hearts and your minds in Christ Jesus.*
PHILIPPIANS 4:6-7

It happens regularly nowadays. A beeper goes off in a room full of people. In response to the beeper, someone gets up, leaves the room, and makes a phone call. Something needed immediate attention, and the phone call took care of it.

Life is full of things that need immediate attention. Problems, frustrations, and distresses can produce anxiety and rob us of peace. God doesn't want this to happen, so he has provided a way that we can get in touch with him immediately when anxiety attacks.

Anxiety is God's beeper system alerting us that it's time to talk to God about a situation that worries us. God invites us to come to him in prayer when anxiety threatens, and he promises that he will restore peace in our lives.

We are welcome to come to God with any request, large or small. Nothing is too great for God's power; nothing is too small for him to care about. If it is a concern to you, it is a concern to God.

We're encouraged to come "with thanksgiving." Thanksgiving arises from remembering who God is and what he does for us. Remember that God is love and that nothing can separate us from his love (1 John 4:16; Romans 8:38-39). Remember that God is mighty and that his strong right arm is our defense (Psalm 60:5). Remember that God's goodness and mercy will follow you all the days of your life (Psalm 23:6), and you will always be thankful (Colossians 2:7).

The result of prayer is peace—"the peace of God, which transcends all understanding"—a peace that is beyond the ability of humans to contrive or produce.

God not only works out for good the situations we place in his hands (Romans 8:28); he also works in us to guard our hearts and minds in Christ Jesus (Philippians 4:7).

Is God beeping you through some concern in your heart or life? Get in touch with him immediately. Don't delay! He'll be glad to have you come. He's invited you. He has a wonderful peace to give you.

Reflect

♦ Think about how you have handled worries and anxiety in the past. Is there some way you can improve your way of handling these things, based on this Scripture passage?

♦ What signs would you look for to confirm that you have handled anxiety in a God-pleasing way?

Pray

♦ *Praise* God—the hearer of prayer, the peace giver, the One who guards your heart and mind in Jesus Christ.

♦ *Ask* God to forgive you for any times you may have handled anxiety improperly.

♦ *Thank* God for the peace he gives in the midst of troubling situations.

♦ *Ask* God to give you peace and to guard your heart and mind.

Act

Identify the one thing that you are most prone to be anxious about. Add it to your petitionary prayer list. Be sure to give thanks for everything God has already done to bless you and to help you deal with that anxiety. (See Appendix D for a "Prayers of Thanksgiving" experience.)

✳

Day Five

When God Says "No"

[7]There was given me a thorn in my flesh, a messenger of Satan, to torment me. [8]Three times I pleaded with the Lord to take it away from me. [9]But he said to me, "My grace is sufficient for you, for my power is made perfect in weakness."

2 CORINTHIANS 12:7-9

Someone has suggested that God answers prayer in the following five ways:

- *"Yes! I thought you would never ask."*
- *"Yes! But not yet."*
- *"No! I love you too much."*
- *"Yes! But different from your thoughts."*
- *"Yes! But more than you ever hoped or dreamed."*

Let's look briefly at each one of these.

"Yes! I thought you would never ask." Here's a reminder that God has so many good things to give us that he can hardly wait till we ask for them. When we finally ask, he is often quick to answer.

"Yes! But not yet." When God asks us to wait, it may seem like a "no" answer. But it's really a delayed "yes." When God delays an answer to prayer, it's always for a good reason. He may be teaching us to depend wholly on him, preparing us to receive the answer when it comes, or simply refining our prayers.

"No! I love you too much." God's wisdom is higher than our wisdom. When what we ask is not good for us, God graciously answers "no." He loves us too much to fulfill our wishes against his better judgment.

"Yes! But different from your thoughts." This also may seem like a "no," but it's really a disguised "yes." Watch carefully for God's answer.

"Yes! But more than you ever hoped or dreamed." What we ask for may

be good and right, but God may choose to give us something even better. He sees the big picture and knows what is really good for us.

One more possible answer needs to be added: *"No! Not until you deal with that sin you are holding on to."* Even that is a gracious answer, for sin, remaining unconfessed and unforgiven, does great harm.

When God said "no" to Paul's request to remove his thorn in the flesh, it was with good reason. By allowing the thorn to remain, God taught Paul about his all-sufficient grace and about his power "made perfect in weakness." In the end Paul came to the point of delighting in weaknesses, insults, hardships, persecutions, and difficulties as he saw God's strength compensating for his weakness (2 Corinthians 12:10).

Our confidence is not in prayer; it is in God. When prayer doesn't seem to work, it doesn't matter so much. God is still our Lord and sustainer who graciously strengthens us.

Reflect

◆ Have you ever been disappointed in God for not answering your prayers? What are some reasons God may have had for not giving what you asked for?

◆ Does it make sense to say, "Our confidence is not in prayer; it is in God"? Why?

Pray

◆ *Praise* God for his all-sufficient grace and power, which he uses on our behalf.

◆ *Confess* any anger you may have toward God if you are disappointed in his way of answering or not answering your prayers.

◆ *Ask* for wisdom to understand God's ways and for grace to be able to delight in God's goodness, even if he says "no" to your requests.

Act

Tell God that you are happy for the times he has said "no" because you know he did it with your best interests in mind.

WEEK FOUR

PRAYING FOR OTHERS

※

Day One

What Is Intercession?

> *⁵Then [Jesus] said to them, "Suppose one of you has a friend, and he goes to him at midnight and says, 'Friend, lend me three loaves of bread, ⁶because a friend of mine on a journey has come to me, and I have nothing to set before him.'*
> *⁷"Then the one inside answers, 'Don't bother me. The door is already locked, and my children are with me in bed. I can't get up and give you anything.' ⁸I tell you, though he will not get up and give him the bread because he is his friend, yet because of the man's boldness he will get up and give him as much as he needs."*
> LUKE 11:5-8

When we move from petition (praying for ourselves) to *intercession* (praying for others), we are shifting the focus of prayer. We need to pray for ourselves so that we may receive all that God intends us to have. We also need to pray for others as an act of self-giving love.

The dictionary defines intercession as "acting between two parties; begging or pleading on behalf of another; mediating." An intercessor is a go-between, representing one party to another. In intercession, believers go before God and make requests on behalf of others.

Jesus' story about the friend-in-the-middle portrays the role of the intercessor. This friend-in-the-middle has a friend-in-need who comes at midnight, and he has a friend-with-bread. Unable to meet the need of his midnight guest, this host goes to his other friend and pleads boldly and shamelessly till he receives what he needs. What he receives he carries back to his friend-in-need. He is a go-between.

The position of the friend-in-the-middle is the position of an intercessor, who pleads with one who has much on behalf of one who has nothing. In other words, intercessors labor before God—the Friend-with-bread—and plead with him on behalf of those who need the bread of heaven.

In the ongoing work of God, intercessory prayer is of prime importance. People desperately need our intercessory prayers. Many people are hurting. Many families are dysfunctional. Many churches are stagnated. Many neighbors are living lonely, isolated lives. The majority of people in North America do not have a saving knowledge of Jesus Christ. And they need far more than we are able to give them.

They need what only God can give. And God chooses to give his good gifts in response to the intercessory prayers of his people. That's where we come in. We can be friends-in-the-middle to God's lost and hurting world.

Reflect

◆ Who in your family, church, or neighborhood is like the friend who came at midnight? What kind of help do they need that is beyond your ability to give?

◆ What are you willing to do to see that they get what they need from God?

Pray

◆ *Praise* God as the all-sufficient giver of every good gift.

◆ *Confess* any failure on your part to intercede faithfully on behalf of needy persons around you.

◆ *Commit* yourself to labor before God on behalf of your family, friends, neighbors, fellow workers, church members, and others.

◆ *Intercede* right now on behalf of one or more needy persons whom God is bringing to mind.

Act

Make a list of persons for whom God would have you intercede on a regular basis. Start with family and friends but go beyond them by asking God to lay certain coworkers, classmates, neighbors and acquaintances on your heart.

✸

Day Two

God Seeks Intercessors

[30]"I looked for a man among them who would build up the wall and stand before me in the gap on behalf of the land [of Israel] so I would not have to destroy it, but I found none. [31]So I will pour out my wrath on them and consume them with my fiery anger, bringing down on their own heads all they have done, declares the Sovereign Lord."
EZEKIEL 22:30-31
(FOR BACKGROUND TO THIS PASSAGE, READ EZEKIEL 22:23-30.)

Several years ago I was making a determined effort to become a better intercessor. I tried to give it more time, cover more needs, and pray with greater intensity. For a while things went well. Soon, however, I found myself skipping these extended prayer times when it wasn't convenient. But it bothered me that I could skip prayer so easily.

When I asked the Lord for insight on this, he helped me see that my problem was that I didn't really believe intercession changed anything. It seemed that life went on normally around me whether I prayed or not.

Then God brought me to Ezekiel 22. He showed me that intercessors, who by means of their prayers "build up the wall and stand . . . in the gap," are absolutely crucial to his government of the world. When I asked the question "Would the history of Israel have been different if God had found an intercessor?" I had to answer "yes." When I asked a further question, "Does the history of my family, church, or neighborhood depend on my intercession?" the answer again was "yes."

God seeks intercessors not because he lacks the wisdom or power to govern the world without them but because he, in his sovereign good pleasure, has chosen to govern the world through the prayers of his people. Intercession is not optional. It is a necessary and important part of God's way of working.

Things will happen when we pray that wouldn't have happened if we hadn't prayed. And things will not happen if we do not pray that would have happened if we had prayed.

In the New Testament era God the Father always finds an intercessor to "build up the wall and stand before [him] in the gap." The One he finds is Jesus Christ, who ever lives to make intercession. But Christ does not pray alone. Our intercessory prayers are coupled with his. And he, by means of his Spirit, prays through us.

No wonder the kingdom is advancing and the gospel is spreading to every nation in the world. It's because of prayer. Are your prayers contributing to this worldwide thrust?

Reflect

- ♦ Try to imagine God determining what will happen in your family, on your block, in your church, or in your nation on the basis of your prayers. How does that make you feel?
- ♦ What does this suggest about the importance of your role as an intercessor?

Pray

- ♦ *Praise* God for the greatness of his power and the wisdom of his choice to govern the world through the prayers of his people.
- ♦ *Confess* any failure at intercession that you are now aware of.
- ♦ *Thank* God for the awesome privilege of ruling the world with God through your prayers of intercession.
- ♦ *Ask* for grace to be a faithful intercessor.

Act

Think of the five letters of the word BLESS to help you remember five important ways to intercede for family, friends, neighbors and coworkers.

- ♦ **B** Body – health, protection, energy, fitness
- ♦ **L** Labor – work, income, security, skills
- ♦ **E** Emotional – joy, peace, grief, anxiety, anger
- ♦ **S** Social – love, marriage, family, friends
- ♦ **S** Spiritual – salvation, grace, faith, hope

✳

Day Three

The Scope of Intercession

*¹I urge, then, first of all, that requests, prayers, intercession
and thanksgiving be made for everyone—²for kings and all those
in authority, that we may live peaceful and quiet lives in all
godliness and holiness. ³This is good, and pleases God our Savior,
⁴who wants all men to be saved and to come to
a knowledge of the truth.*
1 TIMOTHY 2:1-4

E. M. Bounds said, "Prayer can do anything God can do." That's true because the only power in prayer is the power of God. What's more, prayer can reach anywhere God can reach. And God is everywhere, so his power can reach to every corner of the earth through our prayers.

Two phrases in the above verses emphasize the broad scope of prayer: "for everyone" and "all men [people]." Because God wants all people "to be saved and to come to a knowledge of the truth," he urges us to pray for everyone.

Ole Hallesby in his classic book *Prayer* grasps the heart of Paul's injunction: "It is our Lord's will that we who have received access to these powers through prayer should go through this world transmitting heavenly power to every corner of the world which needs it sorely. Our lives should be . . . quiet but steadily flowing streams of blessing, which through our prayers and intercessions should reach our whole environment" (p. 64).

When I sit in my favorite chair for my morning devotions, I imagine my prayers ascending to the throne room of heaven, and I imagine God, in response, moving his hands in the places where my prayers direct. I imagine his power being released on the west coast as I pray for family members, in our nation's capital as I pray for government officials, in foreign lands as I pray for mission enterprises, and in the homes and hearts of my neighbors as I pray for them. My prayers can release a blessing or bring change anywhere in the world without my moving from that chair. What an awesome power God has given us!

Though God would have us pray broad intercessory prayers, our prayer responsibilities start close to home. Our first responsibility is for immediate family members, then relatives and friends, then the spiritual family in which God has placed us, and then beyond that to our neighbors, community, nation, and world.

If our prayers focus only on those who are nearby, we have not caught the scope of what God intends through prayer. If they focus mainly on those far away, we may be guilty of failing to provide for our immediate families and of denying the faith (1 Timothy 5:4, 8).

Reflect

♦ Imagine your prayers transmitting heavenly power and blessing to people in every corner of the world. Think of some of those people and places.

♦ Imagine persons experiencing the joy of being saved and coming to a knowledge of the truth as a result of your prayers.

Pray

♦ *Praise* God, who is everywhere present in the universe.

♦ *Confess* to God your failure if your prayers have been too narrow and limited in comparison to the charge of 1 Timothy 2:1-4.

♦ *Thank* God for the breadth and depth of his concern for the world.

♦ *Commit* yourself to make "requests, prayers, intercession and thanksgiving . . . for everyone," including "kings and all those in authority."

♦ *Pray* that "all the ends of the earth will remember and turn to the Lord, and all the families of the nations will bow down before him" (Psalm 22:27).

Act

Practice the **BLESS** prayer that you learned in yesterday's reading, and expand on each category as the Spirit guides you to pray for people in your circles of influence. (See Appendix A for an expanded version of the B.L.E.S.S. prayer.)

❉

Day Four

Interceding for Those Who Can't Pray for Themselves

[7]The Lord . . . said to Eliphaz the Temanite, "I am angry with you and your two friends . . . . [8]Go to my servant Job and sacrifice a burnt offering for yourselves. My servant Job will pray for you, and I will accept his prayer and not deal with you according to your folly. . . . [9]And the Lord accepted Job's prayer.

JOB 42:7-9

Several recent polls in North America show that about 80 percent of the population do not have a saving relationship with Jesus Christ. That means people do not regularly have access to God's throne of grace. They may try to pray, but they cannot get through to God, since access to the throne is only through Jesus Christ.

That is a horrible, hopeless state to be in—cut off from the One who is the source of all grace and blessing. That was the state in which Eliphaz and his friends found themselves, at least temporarily, when God came to them and said, "My servant Job will pray for you, and I will accept his prayer." This was God's way of saying, "I won't listen to your prayers. You don't have access. You'd better get Job to pray for you."

The word for *intercession* in the original language of the New Testament means "having freedom of access." It was originally a technical term that meant meeting with a king in order to make a request. In the Bible intercession means "making a request of God on behalf of others."

The privilege of access is given to believers not simply so that we may ask for ourselves but also so that we may ask for others, especially those who have no access. God has so much to give them but, having determined long ago to give in response to asking, he withholds his gracious giving until we intercede.

When believers begin to pray seriously for their neighbors, things begin to happen. When members of a church in Bakersfield, California, planted several *Lighthouses of Prayer* in an apartment complex to pray for those who lived there, the manager became a Christian, drug dealers moved out, crime rates went down, many tenants started going to church, several Bible studies started, and ten people made commitments to Christ. The difference was so evident that the police, discovering the reason for the changes, asked the church to consider planting similar *Lighthouses* in other complexes.

What do you think God wants to see happen in the lives of the people around you? Are you willing to be the one to intercede so that God will accomplish his will in your neighborhood through your prayers?

Reflect

- ◆ Try to imagine what it would be like to be a non-Christian with no one to pray for you.
- ◆ Consider what it would mean for you, if you were an unbeliever, to live or work near a believer who would regularly pray for you. Prayer, and the blessing from God that comes through prayer, is a gift you can give to non-Christians around you. Think about it.

Pray

- ◆ *Thank* God for the privilege of access to his throne, opened up for you through Jesus Christ.
- ◆ If you have failed to use your privilege of access to God on behalf of unsaved persons, *confess* this sin and claim God's forgiving grace.
- ◆ *Tell* God of your readiness to be a faithful intercessor, and ask for his help in doing it.

Act

Ask God to make clear to you what he wants to accomplish in the lives of the non-Christians persons or families he has led you to pray for. Wait patiently for God's answer. Pray about the things God brings to mind.

✹

Day Five

Interceding for the Unsaved

*Brothers, my heart's desire and prayer to God for the Israelites
is that they may be saved.*
ROMANS 10:1

The Bible clearly requires us to pray for persons who are not saved. In 1 Timothy 2 we are reminded that God wants all persons to be saved, and we are urged "therefore" to pray for everyone. Jesus modeled prayer for the unsaved when he prayed, "My prayer is not for [my disciples] alone. I pray also for those who will believe in me through their message" (John 17:20). And the apostle Paul was praying for the unsaved when he prayed his heart's desire for the Israelites (Romans 10:1).

How shall we pray for those who are not saved?

First, we should pray that *the unsaved will be drawn by the Father.* Jesus said, "No one can come to me unless the Father who sent me draws him" (John 6:44).

Second, we should pray that *those who hear the gospel will understand it.* Jesus warns that the evil one will come and snatch away the gospel seed sown in a person's heart if it is not understood (Matthew 13:19). The spiritual understanding and enlightenment required must come from God, who is moved to respond to the prayers of his people.

Third, we should pray that *unbelievers' eyes will be opened so that they can see the light.* As we pray this prayer, we will once again be contending with the adversary, "the god of this age [who] has blinded the minds of unbelievers, so that they cannot see the light of the gospel of the glory of Christ" (2 Corinthians 4:4). Opening spiritual eyes is, of course, God's business. But releasing God's power to open blinded eyes is prayer business, to which God calls us.

God honors prayer for the unsaved. A *Lighthouse* in Grand Rapids,

Michigan, prayed for a young man who had run away from home and joined a gang. The young man returned home and made a commitment to Christ. Later his grandfather gave his life to Christ shortly before he died, also in response to prayer.

Another *Lighthouse* in western Michigan saw four families come to the Lord after eight months of weekly meetings to pray for their neighbors.

This is prayer-evangelism, evangelism in which God moves in the hearts and lives of people in response to the earnest prayers of believers. Who among those who will believe in Christ are you praying for?

Reflect

- ◆ Do you care enough about the unsaved to pray earnestly for their salvation?
- ◆ Would you care more if it were your own children or family members who were unsaved? Remember that all unsaved persons are wayward sons and daughters of God's family. God does not want "anyone to perish, but everyone to come to repentance" (2 Peter 3:9).

Pray

- ◆ *Praise* God, who "so loved the world that he gave his one and only Son, that whoever believes in him shall . . . have eternal life" (John 3:16).
- ◆ *Thank* God for those who prayed for you and helped to open the door of salvation for you.
- ◆ If you do not have a burden for the unsaved, *ask* God to put such a burden on your heart.
- ◆ *Commit* yourself to partner with Jesus Christ in praying for persons yet to be saved.

Act

Put the list of unsaved persons for whom you pray in a place where you will see it every day. Pray that the Father will draw them to himself, that they will understand the good news of salvation in Jesus, and will have their eyes opened to the light of God's goodness. Continue to pray for them daily. (See Appendix H for a guide to "Interceding For Unsaved Persons".)

WEEK FIVE

PRAYER AS A WAY OF LIFE

※

Day One

Prayer as a Conversation with God

*Then the man and his wife heard the sound of the Lord God as
he was walking in the garden in the cool of the day, and they hid
from the Lord God among the trees of the garden.*
GENESIS 3:8

It's clear from Genesis 3:8 that God regularly met Adam and Eve in the cool of the evening in order to spend time with them in conversation. It was part of Adam and Eve's regular, perhaps even daily, experience. So on this day when they heard "the sound of the Lord God as he was walking in the garden," they knew it was time for another talk with God.

Prayer is conversation with God. What regularly took place in the Garden of Eden—conversation between God and humans—was prayer. This "prayer" was clearly not a stilted, formal, cliché-filled monologue. I can only imagine it to be a relaxed, uninhibited, informal, two-way conversation. That, I think, is the first and best picture of prayer in the Bible.

What happened there in the garden instructs us about prayer. It shows us first, that God takes the initiative in prayer. It's the Lord who comes to Adam and Eve and calls out. When you feel a desire to pray, it's God who is stirring up that desire in you and inviting you to meet with him. Prayer is essentially a relationship that begins with God.

This garden event also shows us what sin does to prayer. After they sinned, Adam and Eve were reluctant to meet with God. Instead of skipping out to meet their beloved friend, we see them hiding in the bushes, feeling ashamed and guilty. Fear has replaced freedom. Sin put a gulf between God and the first human beings. Conversation couldn't happen with Adam and Eve hiding in the bushes. Sin hinders prayer.

Have you ever felt reluctance in coming to God? At times we are like

Adam and Eve—afraid of God, hiding behind excuses and hesitant to meet him. Unconfessed sin, harbored in the heart, cancels out prayer.

But grace restores prayer. Notice that God doesn't walk away and leave Adam and Eve in their hiding place. Instead he calls them out and graciously helps them come to grips with the sin that has estranged them from him. God initiates the process that leads to forgiveness, to restored fellowship, and to opened channels of communication—to prayer.

From the beginning God intended prayer to be a restful, two-way conversation with him, like that in the garden before sin. God brings us back to that again and again as he comes in grace to meet us each day. God wants to walk and talk with us and to enjoy our company.

When God comes to meet you today, don't hide. Welcome him! Grace has prevailed. In Christ your sins are forgiven. Go out to meet God laughing and skipping. And have a relaxed, informal, dialog that will be a joy for both of you.

Reflect

- ◆ Do you sometimes feel reluctant to pray? If so, what is it that blocks your desire to meet God? Let God help you identify and deal with it.
- ◆ When you pray, are you aware of meeting a real person—a thinking, feeling, willing, acting, talking, listening God?
- ◆ Are you comfortable talking with God in plain language and in ways that are relaxed, informal, and uninhibited?

Pray

- ◆ *Praise* God, who is present with us through his Spirit and eager to converse with us.
- ◆ *Confess* anything that has distanced you from God.
- ◆ *Thank* God for dealing with your sin and eliminating it as a barrier to your relationship with him.
- ◆ *Ask* God for a prayer life built around relaxed, enjoyable, uninhibited daily conversations with him.
- ◆ *Intercede* for people around you whose prayer lives are constricted because they are hiding from God.

Act

Take a pleasant walk at the end of your day and be conscious that Jesus is walking with you. Talk to him as you would to a friend about your day—about things you are thinking, feeling, and doing. Try to imagine what he would say to you.

✹

Day Two

Living Prayerfully

Pray continually.
1 THESSALONIANS 5:17

Praying continually does not mean we are to do nothing but pray. It means that we live all of our hours and days so conscious of God that we are actually, at one level or another, keeping company with him always.

It means *walking and talking with God*. When Enoch, an Old Testament hero of faith, "walked with God," it meant that God was his conscious companion in all of his daily activities (Genesis 5:22). When you travel with a friend, there's a lot to talk about: sights to see, experiences to share, and decisions to make. When you travel through life with God, there's just as much to talk about. And although you cannot physically see or touch God, he is really with you—a thinking, feeling, willing, communicating, listening person.

Praying continually means making it a habit to talk to God about our everyday *experiences*. Repeated activities can become triggers for God-consciousness. The famous American general Stonewall Jackson once commented, "I have so fixed the habit in my mind that I never raise a glass of water to my lips without asking God's blessing, never seal a letter without putting a word of prayer under the seal, never take a letter to the post without a brief sending of my thoughts heavenward, never change my classes in the lecture room without a minute's petition for the cadets who go out and for those who come in."

You probably already have some prayer triggers in your life: rising in the morning, sitting to eat a meal, or lying down to sleep. A friend of mine prays every time he gets behind the wheel of his car. Others have learned to pray for every person they meet, every needful situation that comes on the news, every time they enter their place of work, every time the phone rings, every time they hear a fire siren or see an accident, or every time they pass a church.

Praying continually means sharing our *thoughts* with God. Our minds never lie dormant. No matter what we are doing from morning till night, our minds are always working. The morning news, breakfast on the fly, traffic on the way to work, challenges on the job, dealing with children, connecting with a spouse, relaxing in front of the TV—all engage us mentally in some way. God wants to be in on our thoughts.

Praying continually also means sharing our *feelings* with God. Feelings are spontaneous inner reactions to things we are experiencing in life. God wants to be in on our feelings. That's why the Spirit prompted James to write, "Is any one of you in trouble? He should pray. Is anyone happy? Let him sing songs of praise" (James 5:13).

Try to develop the habit of filling your day with little prayers. Every fresh prayer will bring a sweet inflowing from God.

Reflect

♦ What "prayer triggers" are already present in your life? What triggers will you try to add today?

♦ Do you dare to believe that God really wants to keep company with you? It's true! How does that make you feel?

Pray

♦ *Praise* God as the personal God who enjoys your company and gives you his joy.

♦ *Confess* the bad habit of leaving God out of your thoughts, feelings, and experiences.

♦ *Ask* God for his help to pray continually. This is not something you can do naturally.

♦ *Intercede* for family members, friends, and neighbors, that they may have an increased consciousness of God and a desire to walk and talk with him.

Act

Try to add at least one new prayer trigger each day during the next week.

❈

Day Three

Hearing from Heaven

"My sheep hear my voice, and I know them, and they follow me."
JOHN 10:27 (NKJV)

Prayer is a dialog between the believer and God—a dialog of love. It's two-way communication that involves both talking and listening. That's the kind of prayer relationship God wants with us. Prayer isn't complete if we do all the talking and expect God to do all the listening. True prayer requires both.

When Jesus said, "My sheep hear my voice," he meant that people who are truly believers recognize and respond to his voice. They are constantly tuned in to him and ready to respond to his call. That's the kind of listening that prayer requires.

A tourist traveling early one morning in an eastern country spotted a number of sheep in a fold. Shepherds standing at the gate of the sheepfold were calling their sheep one by one out of the fold and taking them to pasture. "Would you let me call out your sheep?" said the stranger to one of the shepherds. "Sure," said the shepherd, with a smile, and told him what to say. The stranger called for the sheep to come out, using the very words the shepherd had given him. Not a sheep moved, though he called several times. Finally, the shepherd stepped forward and called to his sheep with the same words he had given to the stranger. In response to his call, the sheep came out of the fold and followed him into the fields. They knew his voice.

Prayer is all about hearing our Shepherd's voice. In fact, when we pray, it's probably more important to listen than to speak. After all, God has far more to say than you or I do. Before rushing into God's presence with your thoughts and needs, be attentive to what God is trying to tell you.

Hearing God also means a readiness to obey. God does not speak just to give people a chance to decide if they want to obey. God speaks to those who take him seriously and who stand ready to respond to whatever he says.

When listening, be sure that the voice you hear is the Shepherd's voice. There are other voices clamoring for attention—the voice of the evil one, the voices of the world, and the inner voices of your own selfish desires. The better you know the Shepherd, the more sure you will be of his voice. If you are unsure, ask Jesus to open your ears to his voice and to close your ears to the misleading voices of the enemy. He will be more than happy to do that.

If this kind of listening is new to you, begin by asking the Shepherd to tune your ears to his voice. Be conscious of him. Expect to hear his voice. Be prepared for his voice to break through at any time of the day for any purpose. And be ready to respond.

The Shepherd is eager for you to hear his voice! Are you as eager to listen?

Reflect

- ◆ Who does most of the talking in your prayer life? Does prayer truly mean two-way communication with God?
- ◆ Can you think of times when God has seemed to impress something on you even if you weren't consciously listening? What was God "saying"?
- ◆ Can you honestly say to God, "I will do whatever you say"?

Pray

- ◆ *Praise* the Shepherd, who speaks so that we may hear his voice and follow him.
- ◆ *Thank* God for telling us the truth about himself, about ourselves, and about our world.
- ◆ *Confess* any lack of desire or personal failure in hearing God's voice.
- ◆ *Ask* God to open your heart to his impressions and to close your ears to the whisperings of the evil one.
- ◆ *Intercede* for those who are not listening to God's Word or Spirit and as a result are straying from the truth.

Act

Ask God how he wants you to treat a person with whom you have a troubled relationship. Make a commitment, in advance, to do what God says. Wait in prayerful silence for God's direction. Write down what you think he is saying. Check that against the written Word of God. When you are sure you know what God is saying, do what he says.

❋

Day Four

Praying the Ordinary

Pray in the Spirit on all occasions with all kinds of prayers and requests. With this in mind, be alert and always keep on praying for all the saints.
EPHESIANS 6:18

Did you notice the four "alls" in this passage—"all occasions," "all kinds," "always," and "all the saints"? What a simple way to say that prayer is tremendously important, that *all* of life is to be brought to God in prayer.

Praying begins not with self but with God. To "pray in the Spirit" means to pray with the help of the Spirit, under the influence of the Spirit. It means praying the thoughts that the Spirit kindles within us. What is impossible in our own strength becomes possible with the Spirit's help.

Pray "on all occasions" means that prayer is to be as broad as life itself. Talk to God about your problems, your joys, your temptations, and your struggles. Let him in on your everyday life: your work, your bill paying, leisure time, shopping, visits to the doctor, and time with friends. There is nothing in life than cannot be prayed about. Welcome God right into the middle of your sometimes mundane, usually busy, occasionally stressful, and always complex life. Pray about the ordinary.

Pray "all kinds of prayers." Let there be no blessing without a word of thanks, no sin without expressed confession, no need arising without a prayer of supplication, and no glimpse of God's glory without a whispered prayer of praise. If prayer is the talking part of a love relationship with God, keep up the love relationship by talking with God about all kinds of things.

Pray "always"! This means that prayer is not to be cubby-holed into special times and special days. It never needs to be put off. There is never a better time to pray than at any given moment. Prayer is meant to be a natural, ongoing part of all our days and nights.

Also be sure to "pray for all the saints." This isn't possible if it means praying for every Christian in the world by name. But you can pray specifically for Christians you know—family members, friends, fellow church members, neighbors. It also works to pray by categories—for church leaders, persecuted Christians, Christians in power, Christians in media, believers of different ethnic backgrounds, Christians in specific countries with great needs.

Because of prayer the weakest Christian does not have to fear "the devil's schemes" or all "the powers of this dark world and . . . the spiritual forces of evil" (Ephesians 6:11-12). Every true believer can live in constant fellowship with the mightiest ally in the world—God himself. In him we have the strength to stand. Prayer is the God-given way our relationship with God is maintained.

Reflect

- ◆ Review the past 24 hours of your life. Can you think of one glimpse of God's glory that deserved praise, one gift that deserved a word of thanks, one sin that needs to be confessed, or one need that begs for God's help? Are you talking to God about these things?
- ◆ What "saints" (other Christians) need your prayers right now in order to stand against the devil's schemes?

Pray

- ◆ *Praise* the Spirit of God, who alone knows the thoughts of God and is able to reveal them to us.
- ◆ *Thank* the Spirit for helping us pray as we ought and for kindling in our hearts prayers that are pleasing to God.
- ◆ *Confess* any failure you are aware of to pray all kinds of prayers on all occasions and to always keep on praying for all the saints.
- ◆ *Ask* for the Spirit's help to be conscious of and talking to God throughout the day in all circumstances.
- ◆ *Intercede* in behalf of other Christians who need your prayers to be able to be stand in the face of the devil's schemes.

Act

Whenever you start to pray, whether at set-aside times or on the run, stop and ask the Holy Spirit to direct your prayers and give you the right thoughts and words. (See Appendix B for an experience in praying "all kinds of prayer".)

✹

Day Five

A Private Meeting with
the Father

*"When you pray, go into your room, close the door and pray to
your Father, who is unseen. Then your Father, who sees what is
done in secret, will reward you."*
MATTHEW 6:6

Few things in life are more precious than time spent alone with God.
The purpose of time spent with God is to build a deeper personal
relationship with him. Within the seclusion of our private prayer lives,
as we spend time with the Lord, we grow in love for him and are transformed more and more into the image of Christ.

When Jesus says, "Go into your room, close the door and pray to your
Father," he is saying, "Go to a private place where you can withdraw and
commune with God in prayer." Today we call such a private meeting with
God daily devotions.

Many of the great saints of Scripture model this practice. David prayed
every morning (Psalm 5:3). Daniel prayed three times each day (Daniel
6:10). Anna and Simeon prayed daily in the temple (Luke 2:25, 36-37).
Paul prayed constantly for the new believers in the churches he founded.
Jesus, who had perfect fellowship with the Father, found it important to
have private times to commune with him. Luke reports that "Jesus often
withdrew to lonely places and prayed" (Luke 5:16). The people I know
who have the most vibrant faith have, like these devoted pray-ers, built
their spiritual lives around a consistent time spent with God.

A disciplined daily devotional life is not optional for a growing
Christian. It's a must. Prayer is the conversational part of a love relation-

ship with God. You don't build a love relationship by staying away from the other person. Love relationships are built by spending time together. God wants us to have a close relationship with him. When we do, we are the winners. God fills us with joy in his presence (Psalm 16:11).

But personal devotions are not simply a matter of *our* wanting and needing to spend time with God. *He desires* to spend time with us too—as much time as possible. God took great joy in creating us and saving us. He knows us and loves us. He enjoys expressing his love to us as we spend time with him. We are important to him. David says, "The Lord has set apart the godly for himself" (Psalm 4:3). Zephaniah declares that God takes "great delight" in us, quiets us "with his love," and rejoices over us with singing (Zephaniah 3:17). Our daily time with God is a time for him to shower love on us. This gives God great pleasure. It can give us great pleasure too. That's part of the reward.

I have never met a person who regrets the time set aside for a private daily meeting with the Lord. Are you among this crowd?

Reflect

◆ How are you responding to Christ's command to "go into your room, close the door and pray to your Father"? Are you getting the "reward" he promised?

◆ Try to imagine the look on God's face as he takes great delight in you. What do you suppose God does to quiet you with his love? Can you "hear" God's song as he rejoices over you?

Pray

◆ *Praise* God for his great love—a love for you, a person whom he knows by name.

◆ *Thank* God for giving you the opportunity to meet him privately anytime you choose, and thank him for his readiness to meet you.

◆ *Confess* any reluctance in your relationship with God that causes you to hold back.

◆ *Ask* for God's help and guidance to improve on your personal devotional life.

◆ *Intercede* for family members and friends who need to spend more time with the Lord.

Act

Establish a *time* to meet God each day. Decide on a *place* where you can meet God in private. Make a *commitment* that is an appropriate response to Jesus' words in Matthew 6:6. Act on your plan within the next 24 hours.

WEEK SIX

MODEL PRAYERS OF THE BIBLE

❋

Day One

Our Lord's Model Prayer

⁹"This, then is how you should pray: 'Our Father in heaven, hallowed be your name, ¹⁰your kingdom come, your will be done on earth as it is in heaven. ¹¹Give us today our daily bread. ¹²Forgive us our debts, as we also have forgiven our debtors. ¹³And lead us not into temptation, but deliver us from the evil one.'"

MATTHEW 6:9-13

We call this the Lord's Prayer, but it is actually the disciples' prayer. We know this because Jesus never needed to pray for the forgiveness of sins, as he teaches us to do in this passage.

This is truly a *model* prayer. Jesus didn't say, "This is *what* you should pray." He said, "This is *how* you should pray." This prayer wasn't meant to be mechanically repeated. Of course, it is not wrong to use the actual words as a prayer, as long as they are prayed from the heart.

The opening words, "Our Father in heaven," settle the issue of our relationship to God. The One we address is indeed "in heaven"—the mighty, majestic, sovereign God of the universe. But to his children who come to him in prayer, God is a loving Father.

This model prayer contains six petitions—the first three are concerns focusing on God; the second three are concerns focusing on human beings. This ordering of petitions reminds us that God should have first place in our life of prayer.

What may be most surprising about the first three petitions is that God wants us to pray about concerns that focus on him. God is perfectly capable of hallowing his name, advancing his kingdom, and enforcing his will without our asking him to do so. But God chooses to operate in response to our prayers. So much is this so that he asks us to pray for these, his greatest concerns, so that he can glorify his name, bring in his kingdom, and enforce his will in answer to our prayers. That makes our prayers tremendously important.

When we ask God to hallow his name, we are asking God to move in this world in ways that will bring him glory and honor. "Your kingdom come" is a prayer for God to establish his reign in people's hearts and minds. "Your will be done on earth as it is in heaven" asks God to help people submit to his will as willingly and completely as the angels in heaven do.

Petitions four, five, and six focus on personal human needs. That Jesus taught us to pray, "Give us today our daily bread," reminds us that God cares about our bodies and wants to provide for our physical needs in response to our asking. "Forgive us our debts" is the prayer of Christians who, having come into a wonderful new relationship with God, want to be rid of any sin that might hinder that relationship. "Lead us not into temptation" is a prayer that God will sustain us in the face of temptations that come from the forces of evil in this world and try to lure us away from God.

To his disciples Jesus said, "This, then, is how you should pray." Are you his disciple? Then this is how you should pray!

Reflect

♦ Does the order of your prayer life reflect the God-first order of the Lord's Prayer? What percentage of your prayer time is spent on concerns that focus on God?

♦ Do you care enough about God's glory, his kingdom, and his will to pray these petitions from the heart?

♦ Can you believe that God might *not* glorify his name, advance his kingdom, or enforce his will in certain instances just because you didn't pray?

Pray

The best way to use a model prayer is to take the core idea in each petition and to expand upon it. Try to do this now in a prayer spending a couple of minutes with each petition.

Act

Pray an expanded version of the Lord's Prayer daily for the next week and imagine some ways in which God is responding to your petitions. Imagine God, for example, making his presence felt in a worship service (hallowing), blessing crops with rain and sunshine (giving bread), and giving Christians the strength to resist temptations.

✤

Day Two

A Ladder of Prayer

[14]For this reason I kneel before the Father, [15]from whom his whole family in heaven and on earth derives its name. [16]I pray that out of his glorious riches he may strengthen you with power through his Spirit in your inner being, [17]so that Christ may dwell in your hearts through faith. And I pray that you, being rooted and established in love, [18]may have power, together with all the saints, to grasp how wide and long and high and deep is the love of Christ, [19]and to know this love that surpasses knowledge—that you may be filled to the measure of the fullness of God.
EPHESIANS 3:14-19

Paul's bracing prayer for the family of God gives us an outline of how to pray for others—a prayer ladder to ascend. There are six steps:

1. *Pray for inner strength by the power of the Holy Spirit.* Proverbs 4:23 calls the heart "the wellspring of life." And Jesus taught that "the good man brings good things out of the good stored up in his heart" and warned that "the evil man brings evil things out of the evil stored up in his heart" (Luke 6:45). What happens in the inner person is of crucial importance. Our prayers are able to affect what happens in other believers.

2. *Pray that Christ may live in believers' hearts through faith.* Christ desires to live and act on earth today in and through believers. He does so to the degree that they yield to his promptings and have his mind, his will, his vision, his courage, his love, and his power. When we pray this way for others, we ask that Christ may more and more live in us and accomplish his will through us.

3. *Pray that believers will be grounded in God's love.* The people we pray for need to be rooted in love, nourished by God's love as a plant is nourished by its roots. They need to be established in love, to have God's love as the solid foundation of their lives.

4. *Pray that believers grasp the scope of Christ's love*—that is, to grasp "how wide and long and high and deep" it is. An unknown prisoner

reached for the meaning of this phrase when he wrote,

Could we with ink the oceans fill
And were the skies of parchment made,
Were every stalk on earth a quill
And every man a scribe by trade—
To write the love of God above
Would drain the oceans dry;
Nor could the scroll contain the whole
Though stretched from sky to sky.

5. *Pray that believers may experience the love of Christ.* It's wonderful if the people we pray for grasp the scope of Christ's love. It's even more important for them to experience it. That's what we ask when we pray for them "to know this love that surpasses knowledge." This is the "knowing" of a personal relationship.

6. *Pray that believers may be filled with the very nature of God.* In these words Paul's ladder of prayer reaches its highest rung. To pray for a filling "to the measure of all the fullness of God" is to ask God to pour himself into us, the children of his earthly family, with a spiritual fullness like God himself possesses.

What more could we ask as we pray for others? Have you asked God for these things for others, and for yourself?

Reflect

- How much effort do you invest in praying for the spiritual well-being of others? What will it take for you to become more like Paul in your intercessory prayers?
- What difference do you expect to see as you pray in this way for the people around you?

Pray

- *Praise* God for his power and love, which alone make this kind of prayer possible.
- *Confess* any failure in prayer that this passage makes you aware of.
- *Ask* God for a greater comprehension of his power and love so that it will be natural for you to pray these requests for others.
- *Thank* God that he loves you and is willing and able to pour his fullness into you.

Act

Using the ladder of prayer, *intercede* for people whom God has placed on your heart.

❋

Day Three

A Prayer for Spiritual Riches

> [9]. . . We have not stopped praying for you and asking God to fill
> you with the knowledge of his will through all spiritual wisdom
> and understanding. [10]And we pray this in order that you may live
> a life worthy of the Lord and may please him in every way: bear-
> ing fruit in every good work, growing in the knowledge of God,
> [11]being strengthened with all power according to his glorious
> might so that you may have great endurance and patience, and
> joyfully [12]giving thanks to the Father.
> COLOSSIANS 1:9-12

Some years ago this great prayer of Paul for the Colossian Christians took me on a prayer journey. It began as I contemplated the amazing depth and scope of Paul's prayer for the Colossians and thought, "It sure would be great to have Paul as a prayer partner." Then it occurred to me that if I prayed for these blessings for myself, God would surely grant what I asked, since these are all in line with his will. I began immediately to claim them.

Then I thought, "I can't have Paul praying these things for me, but *I can be the one* who prays them for *others*. So I began to pray these petitions regularly for my wife and children, as well as for other family members and friends.

What impresses me most is that these intercessory requests are all spiritual in nature. There is no prayer here for the physical or material concerns of life. Of course, we should pray for physical things like health, energy, and protection. But in Paul's praying the spiritual blessings clearly overshadow the physical.

Try to imagine, for example, what would happen in a person's spiritual life if everything the person asked for in prayer were granted in increasing measure. He or she would be

- growing deeper day by day in the knowledge of God's will
- applying biblical principles to daily living by the wisdom and insight

of the Holy Spirit
- living an exemplary Christian life that brings credit to Jesus Christ and joy to God's heart
- engaging in all kinds of fruitful ministry activities
- continuing to grow deeper in the knowledge of God
- enduring with joy and patience the toughest of life experiences by the awesome power of God within
- joyfully giving thanks to God the Father, all the while looking confidently forward to life in the new and glorious kingdom of light.

Wow! I'd sure like to be that person, wouldn't you? So would many believers who live and work near you—and your prayers can help make this a reality for them.

I am sure that Paul's prayers made a real difference in the Colossian congregation he prayed for. God, you see, is eager to answer these kinds of prayers because what is being prayed for is exactly what God wants to see happening in our lives and in the church.

Aren't there some folks you would like to bless in this way?

Reflect

- ◆ Are the kinds of things Paul prays for in Colossians 1:9-12 the kinds of things you *really, truly* want in your life? If so, then ask for them, not just now and then, but every day.
- ◆ Imagine what would happen in your family or your congregation if every person were prayed for each day with a prayer like Paul's Colossian prayer. Is there some way to make that happen?

Pray

- ◆ *Praise* the graciousness of God, who is willing and able to bless us with every spiritual blessing in the heavenly places.
- ◆ *Thank* God for giving us prayer as the means for bringing his blessings to others and ourselves.
- ◆ Have you sinned by failing to pray for persons you know (1 Samuel 12:23)? If so *confess* this to God and start afresh today.
- ◆ *Ask* God to do for you the things Paul prayed for the Colossians.
- ◆ Using this pattern, *intercede* for your children, grandchildren, parents, friends, or other loved ones.

Act

Memorize Colossians 1:9-12 so that you can pray these verses daily without having to refer back to the text. As you pray these prayer themes, try to expand on them and tailor them to specific persons and situations.

❋

Day Four

A Prayer to Know God Better

¹⁷I keep asking that the God of our Lord Jesus Christ, the glorious Father, may give you the Spirit of wisdom and revelation, so that you may know him better. ¹⁸I pray also that the eyes of your heart may be enlightened in order that you may know the hope to which he has called you, the riches of his glorious inheritance in the saints, ¹⁹and his incomparably great power for us who believe.
EPHESIANS 1:17-19

Paul believed that the greatest need of the Ephesian Christians was to know God better. That may also be the greatest need in the church today. One important way Paul worked to help make this happen was to pray for it to happen.

Paul starts by telling us whom he prays to—"the God of our Lord Jesus Christ, the glorious Father." Our confidence when praying is not in prayer itself but in the One to whom we pray—our Father in heaven. Good fathers by their very nature want to love, to protect, to provide, to guide, and to embrace their sons and daughters. It's the nature of our heavenly Father to do all of these things, and God does them to perfection. That's why we can come to God with absolute confidence.

Paul's entire prayer here is about helping people we know and love to know God better. Don't be satisfied for your loved ones simply to know about the Bible, or about God, or even to know God a little. Pray this model prayer for them, asking the Father to help them "know him better." Knowing about God and knowing God are not the same as knowing God well.

Knowing God well means knowing what God is really like—how he thinks, what he wills, how he works, and how he feels about you. It means knowing what gives God pleasure and what evokes his wrath. It means wanting what God wants. It means sharing God's joys and his pain.

What Paul asked for in order to make this happen was "the Spirit of wisdom and revelation." The Spirit knows God perfectly and is the one who can help us know God better and better, for the Spirit lives in our hearts.

People who know God well have "the eyes of their hearts enlightened" to know these things:

1. "The hope to which he has called [them]." When the Bible uses the word "hope," it doesn't mean a strong wish or desire as in common speech today. It means being absolutely certain because God has promised it. Knowing God gives us a certainty about where we are going. It gives us "hope."

2. "The riches of his glorious inheritance in the saints." To know God well is not only to be certain where we will spend eternity but also to know just how good it will be—a glorious inheritance.

3. "His incomparably great power for us who believe." To know God well is to know his great power by experience, to lean on it, to feel it, and to have it coursing through our veins as we live for God in the midst of a crooked and perverse worldly culture.

Is this what you want for yourself and for the people you intercede for? Then ask the Father for these things. He'll hear!

Reflect

◆ How well do you know God? As a starting point, think about a person you know really well, and compare your "knowing" God to the way you know that other person.

◆ How would you go about getting to know God better? What place does prayer have in that process?

◆ Spend some time thinking about the hope of your future, the riches you will inherit, and God's great power at work in you.

Pray

◆ *Praise* "the Spirit of wisdom and revelation" for what he knows and for his willingness to reveal it to you and to the people you pray for.

◆ *Thank* God for his willingness to use his "incomparably great power" to secure your salvation now and for eternity.

◆ If you have made little effort to "know him better," *confess* that to God and ask his forgiveness. Claim the forgiveness that God freely offers you.

◆ *Ask* "the glorious Father" to help you and those you love to "know him better."

Act

Decide what you will personally do to get to know God better. Could that include things like reading and studying God's Word, being part of a Bible study group, taking a personal spiritual retreat, going to church, reading helpful Christian literature?

✳

Day Five

The Prayer of Jabez

Jabez cried out to the God of Israel, "Oh, that you would bless
me and enlarge my territory! Let your hand be with me, and
keep me from harm so that I will be free from pain."
And God granted his request.
1 CHRONICLES 4:10

Jabez's prayer is a daring model of a prayer that we can pray for ourselves as well as for others.

Bruce Wilkinson's book *The Prayer of Jabez* has done much to popularize this prayer in the evangelical world today. Since its publication I have met several Christians who, after reading this book, have learned to pray this prayer for themselves and have experienced surprising answers.

When we sincerely ask for ourselves the very things God wants for us, he is ready to answer. The fact that God "granted his request" confirms that Jabez's prayer was sincere and in line with God's will.

Jabez was a man who believed in prayer. His life was changed through prayer. He asked for four things. His first prayer was, "Oh, that you would bless me." God really does want to bless us, but he wants to do it in response to our asking. That's the way God chooses to work. So when Jabez prayed, "Oh, that you would bless me," God was pleased with that prayer and sent his blessing.

Second, Jabez prayed, ". . . and enlarge my territory." At first this may sound like a greedy desire for material prosperity. But if it had been, I don't think God would have granted it. People who pray wrongly motivated prayers do not get "yes" answers (James 4:3). In Jabez's case, this was a prayer for the restoration of his lost inheritance, which God had promised for all his people. For us to pray for "enlarged territory" probably means praying for the opportunity to break out of whatever is limiting us from being free to live entirely within God's promises for us. That's always a good prayer.

Third, Jabez prayed, "Let your hand be with me." God's hand represents his ability to strengthen and his readiness to act on behalf of his loved ones. Jabez was saying, "Lord, as you enlarge my territory and give me opportunity to serve you, I can't do that in my own strength, so please help me." This is the prayer of a humble person who knows that his strength is in the Lord.

Fourth, Jabez prayed, ". . . and keep me from harm." The greatest source of harm in this world is Satan. This part of Jabez's prayer is similar to the last petition of the Lord's Prayer: "lead us not into temptation, but deliver us from the evil one" (Matthew 6:13).

The passage ends with the astounding declaration "And God granted his request." God did this because he was pleased with Jabez's prayer. He will also be pleased if you pray such a prayer for yourself—not just once, but again and again each day. You see, God wants to bless you; God wants to enlarge your opportunities for service; God wants to strengthen you; God wants to protect you from evil. But, he wants to do all these things in response to your asking. This prayer may be, as Bruce Wilkinson has said, "the key to a life of extraordinary favor with God."

Reflect
- Are the four things Jabez prayed for things that you want in your life so much that you are ready to ask for them again and again?
- What difference would it make if you were to ask for and receive a greater measure of these blessings from God?
- Is there a selfish way to pray this prayer? What would keep this from being a selfish prayer?

Pray
- *Praise* God, who hears and answers prayers that are in line with his will.
- *Thank* God for the blessings, opportunities for service, strength, and protection he has given you in the past.
- *Confess* any spiritual lethargy or laziness that has kept you from realizing your full potential in God's kingdom.
- *Ask* God for every spiritual blessing, for ministry opportunities as large as you can handle, for empowerment in service, and for protection from the evil one.

Act
Tell God that you are available to serve him anytime, any place, doing anything he chooses for you to do, so long as it's clear that the assignment is from him.

WEEK SEVEN

HEROES OF PRAYER

WEEK SEVEN

❋

Day One

Jesus, Man of Prayer

*Very early in the morning, while it was still dark Jesus got up, left
the house and went off to a solitary place, where he prayed.*
MARK 1:35

Jesus often withdrew to lonely places and prayed.
LUKE 5:16

*Jesus went out to a mountainside to pray, and spent
the night praying to God.*
LUKE 6:12

No person every prayed as Jesus did. Prayer was absolutely central
to everything in Jesus' life. E. M. Bounds says of Jesus, "Prayer was
the secret of his power, the law of his life, the inspiration of his toil, and
the source of his wealth, his joy, his communion, and his strength." The
gospels contain no less than 18 references to Jesus' prayer life, 14 distinct
prayer themes on which he taught, and 8 actual prayers.

In some ways it is surprising to think that prayer was necessary for
Jesus. After all, he is the Son of God, the very one who today hears and
answers our prayers. But prayer was necessary for Jesus during the days
of his ministry on earth because he was truly human and shared wholly
in our humanity, except that he did not sin. In taking our limitations on
himself, he accepted even the limitation of depending on the Father and
having to communicate with God in prayer.

Jesus clearly loved to pray. For him it was a lifestyle. He prayed at every
major milestone of his life: at his baptism in the river Jordan, before calling his disciples, before being transfigured, before the Lord's Supper,
before the cross, on the cross, as he died, and before he ascended into
heaven. Jesus prayed at moments of joy (Luke 10:21) and when his heart
was troubled (John 12:27-28). He gained victories in advance through

prayer (John 11:41-42) and averted temptation after his victories through prayer (John 6:15). He prayed so much that he had a reputation as a man of prayer (Matthew 19:13).

Jesus' prayer life was full of variety. He prayed early in the morning, at the end of a long day, and often in between. He prayed in solitary places, on mountainsides, in the wilderness, in a garden, and indoors. One time he is described as kneeling in prayer (Luke 22:41), at another time prostrate (Matthew 26:39), and at another time standing with eyes fixed on heaven (John 11:41). He prayed in private (Luke 9:18) and in public (John 11:41-42).

Jesus also knew how to listen in prayer. In John 7:16 he says, "My teaching . . . comes from him who sent me." And later he noted that the Father commanded him "what to say and how to say it," and that whatever he said was just what the Father had told him to say (John 12:49-50).

Jesus' prayer life did not end with his earthly journey. Today he "is at the right hand of God and is also interceding for us" (Romans 8:34). And "because he always lives to intercede" for us, he is able to save us completely (Hebrews 7:25).

Do you want to be like Jesus? Then learn to pray like Jesus! There is no better way to pray.

Reflect

♦ If someone wrote a brief history of your life, would prayer be a prominent theme in it? Consider what areas of your prayer life most need improving if you are to become more like Jesus.

♦ What kind of priority do you think Jesus wants prayer to have in your life?

Pray

♦ *Praise* Jesus for modeling a strong, positive pattern of prayer for us.

♦ *Confess* any shortcoming in prayer that you are aware of by comparing your prayer life to that of Jesus.

♦ *Thank* the Holy Spirit for his ability and willingness to purify our prayers and to help us when we don't know how to pray very well (Romans 8:26).

♦ *Ask* Christ for the grace to pray as he prayed.

Act

Read and meditate on the Scripture passages referenced in today's devotional reading. As you read each reference, ask the Lord what he wants you to learn from it and to take into your own prayer life.

✹

Day Two

Paul, the Man
Who Prayed Constantly

*⁹God . . . is my witness how constantly I remember you
¹⁰in my prayers at all times.*
ROMANS 1:9-10

*³We always thank God, the Father of our Lord Jesus Christ, when
we pray for you . . . [and] ⁹we have not stopped praying for you.*
COLOSSIANS 1:3, 9

*I thank God, whom I serve . . . as night and day I constantly
remember you in my prayers.*
2 TIMOTHY 1:3

For me, the apostle Paul is a truly great hero of prayer, second only to
Jesus Christ. In studying the pattern of his prayer life, I was amazed
to find no less than 12 distinct passages in Paul's letters in which he uses
"time" words such as *constantly, always, not stopped, every time,* and *night
and day* to describe his prayers for others. What a great example of his
own injunction to "pray continually" (1 Thessalonians 5:17).

One reason Paul prayed so constantly was to express his gratitude to
God for other believers. Again and again Paul begins his letters with words
like "I always thank God for you" and "How can we thank God enough
for you?" Notice also that Paul thanked *God* for these people rather than
just thanking *them.* I like to be thanked, but it is even nicer to have someone thank God for me. That way God gets the credit he deserves, and I
receive the affirmation and joy that go with serving God.

Paul also prayed constantly because he cared so deeply for the people
he prayed for. We sense Paul's caring in statements like "I have you in
my heart" and "I long for all of you with the affection of Christ Jesus"
(Phil. 1:7-8). Deep love tends to elicit constant, heartfelt prayers. A young
man once complained to me that my congregational prayers in worship

services were boring. I asked him if he was bored when I prayed for his grandmother. "No," he said, "then I really tuned in." He caught my point and admitted that he was bored because he didn't really care about the other persons being prayed for. Love gives birth to prayer.

Paul also knew that his prayers would make a huge difference in the lives of his "sons and daughters" in the faith. He prayed so that they would increase and overflow with love for each other (1 Thessalonians 3:12), be enlightened in their hearts, be filled with all the fullness of God (Ephesians 1:18; 3:19), abound in knowledge and depth of insight (Philippians 1:9), and live lives worthy of the Lord (Colossians 1:10). God heard and answered. Paul's prayers accomplished their purpose.

Finally, Paul knew that he needed the prayer support of others. "Join me in my struggle by praying to God for me," he writes in Romans 15:30. "Pray also for me, that whenever I open my mouth, words may be given me," he asks in Ephesians 6:19. And "I know that through your prayers and the help given by the Spirit of Jesus Christ, what has happened to me will turn out for my deliverance," he assures his friends in Philippians 1:19.

Paul the great pray-er is also the one who said, "I urge you to imitate me," and, "Follow my example, as I follow the example of Christ" (1 Corinthians 4:16; 11:1). For this we need much grace.

Reflect
♦ What most impresses you about Paul's prayer life?
♦ What elements of Paul's prayer life do you most need to incorporate into your own prayer life?
♦ Do you personally welcome the prayer support of others for your own spiritual growth and ministry activities?

Pray
♦ *Thank* God for others in your family, or circle of friends. Tell God the specific things about them for which you are thankful.
♦ Does praying for others often bore you? Is it possibly because you don't love them very much? If so *confess* that.
♦ *Pray* for an increase in your ability to see good in others, for a deep sense of care for the well-being of others, and for the confidence that your prayers will make a difference in their lives.

Act
Read the following additional Bible passages that speak of Paul's prayer life: 1 Corinthians 1:4; Ephesians 1:16; 3:14; Philippians 1:3-8; 1 Thessalonians 1:2; 3:9-10; 2 Thessalonians 1:3, 11; Philemon 4. Consider their implications for you.

✸

Day Three

Elijah, An Ordinary Man Who Prayed Powerfully

[17]Elijah was a man like us. He prayed earnestly that it would not rain, and it did not rain on the land for three and a half years. [18]Again he prayed, and the heavens gave rain, and the earth produced its crops.

JAMES 5:17-18

(READ THE FULL STORY OF ELIJAH'S PRAYER VICTORY IN 1 KINGS 17-18.)

When we meet a man of prayer like Elijah, it's tempting to think, "I could never pray like that." But James, in citing Elijah as an example of powerful prayer, dispels that kind of thinking with his comment that "Elijah was a man like us." James is saying that if Elijah, an ordinary person, could pray powerfully, so can we.

This is so because the power of prayer is not in the person or in the words of the prayer. All the power in prayer is God's power released through prayer. It was God who held back the rain for three and a half years, and it was God who caused the rain to return. Yet prayer played a part. It was the prayers of Elijah that moved God's hands. This ordinary man prayed—and look what happened! God still acts in response to the prayers of ordinary people.

Sometimes the prayers of ordinary people are prayers of simple faith uttered quietly and confidently. That was the case as Elijah faced off with the prophets of Baal (1 Kings 18:16-39). After the false prophets had implored their god Baal with shouts, dancing, bloodletting, and failed to get a response, Elijah stepped forward and simply prayed, "O Lord, God of Abraham, Isaac and Israel, let it be known today that you are God in Israel and that I am your servant and have done all these things at your command. Answer me, O Lord, answer me, so these people will know that you, O Lord, are God, and that you are turning their hearts back again." With that simple prayer, fire fell from heaven and consumed Elijah's sacrifice and the wood and stones and even the water in a trench around his altar!

This is not to say that any feeble, superficial, halfhearted prayer will be powerful and effective. James also makes the point that Elijah "prayed earnestly." Earnest prayer gained the results. And that earnest prayer illustrated James's point that, in the words of the J.B. Philips translation, "tremendous power is made available through a good man's earnest prayer."

The prayers of ordinary people also need to be persistent. In order to cause the rain to come again, Elijah went to the top of Mount Carmel and prayed persistently. Time after time he sent his servant to check the horizon for signs of a cloud that would be evidence of answered prayer. Not until the seventh time, when the servant said he saw a cloud rising over the sea "as small as a man's hand," did Elijah stop praying and head down the mountain.

Is there something that God wants to accomplish through your prayers? Why not ask him—earnestly and persistently—and watch for the results.

Reflect

♦ Have you ever felt that you could not pray powerfully like some "super-Christians" you are aware of? What would James say to that?

♦ Have you ever given up on prayer after praying half a dozen times about something? What if Elijah had given up after six prayer efforts?

♦ Review some or your recent prayers. Were they "earnest," or were they halfhearted?

Pray

♦ *Praise* God for the power that makes powerful praying possible.

♦ *Thank* God that he hears and answers the prayers of ordinary persons and makes it possible for us to pray powerfully.

♦ *Ask* God to reveal to you what he wants you to pray about and to help you pray earnestly and persistently.

♦ *Pray* that God will cause his church to grow strong in prayer and be effective in ministry.

Act

Tell God that you are available to pray earnestly and persistently about anything that he lays on your heart, even if it is major and climactic. Listen for God's direction.

✸

Day Four

Jehoshaphat: Victory Through Prayer

> [6]"O Lord, God of our fathers, are you not the God who is in heaven? You rule over the kingdoms of the nations. Power and might are in your hand, and no one can withstand you. . . . [12]We have no power to face this vast army that is attacking us. We do not know what to do, but our eyes are upon you."
>
> 2 CHRONICLES 20:6, 12
>
> (READ THE FULL STORY OF THIS VICTORY THROUGH PRAYER IN
> 2 CHRONICLES 20:1-30.)

Jehoshaphat ranks very near the top of my heroes of prayer list. His prayer leadership won the day when Israel was under attack by a large coalition army of three neighboring nations.

The first thing Jehoshaphat did when faced with a dire threat was to call for a fast. Serious prayer was always part of fasting. Then, standing before the people who had come from every town in Judah, he led them in a most remarkable prayer—a prayer that acknowledged God's adequacy and their human inadequacy. It began with the words "Power and might are in your hand" and ended with these words: "We have no power . . . . We do not know what to do." That's always a good place to start and a good place to end when facing a crisis. Humble prayer is our supreme weapon against the devil's schemes.

Then Jehoshaphat "hears" a word from Lord, who speaks to him and the people through a prophet: "Listen . . . 'Do not be afraid or discouraged because of this vast army. For the battle is not yours, but God's'" (2 Chronicles 20:15). Jehoshaphat didn't have a clue how God was going to fight the battle, but he trusted that God would do what he promised. God's word is always trustworthy.

We know Jehoshaphat and the people trusted God because from that moment on they stopped asking and started praising. "All the people . . . fell down in worship before the Lord" (20:18). If you really believe God's promises, praise is the only proper response.

So thoroughly did Jehoshaphat and the people trust the Lord that they did what was militarily unthinkable; they put a choir at the head of the army. The choir led the army praising God for the splendor of his holiness and singing, "Give thanks to the Lord, for his love endures forever" (20:21). Those who really trust God do not always do things in a conventional way.

As the people marched out praising God, before they ever reach the battle lines, the Lord, true to his promise, confused the enemy so completely that they ended up destroying themselves. God, moving in response to the prayers of his people, always delivers what he promises. That's the confidence we have when we pray.

This remarkable prayer experience of Jehoshaphat and the people of Israel ended where it began, in the temple, with another praise service.

There is only one successful way to face a crisis and to defeat the enemy who wants to triumph over us, and that is through prayer—but not just any old prayer. This kind of victory calls for prayer that begins with, moves out obediently with, and ends with praise.

Reflect

♦ How much time do you spend in praise? Have you ever started, continued, and ended a prayer with praise as Jehoshaphat did?

♦ Have you ever been so sure of God's intervention that you stopped asking and just started praising? Praise has a way of focusing our eyes on God and encouraging trust.

Pray

♦ *Praise* God for the power and might that are in his hand, and that no one can withstand him.

♦ *Thank* God for his readiness to hear prayer and to deliver those who trust in him.

♦ If you have neglected praise *confess* that to God.

♦ *Ask* God for a praising heart.

♦ *Pray* that the church of Jesus Christ, facing major enemies rallied by the evil one, may be delivered.

Act

Read 2 Chronicles 20:1-30. Note that it was Jehoshaphat's knowledge of God and of his victories and promises of the past that gave him boldness in prayer. What do you know about the nature, activities, and promises of God that can undergird your prayers?

✳

Day Five

David: Finding Renewal Through Confession

⁷Cleanse me with hyssop, and I will be clean; wash me, and I will be whiter than snow. ⁸Let me hear joy and gladness; let the bones you have crushed rejoice. ⁹Hide your face from my sins and blot out all my iniquity. ¹⁰Create in me a pure heart, O God, and renew a steadfast spirit within me.

PSALM 51:7-10
(FOR BACKGROUND TO THIS CONFESSION,
READ 2 SAMUEL 11-12 AND PSALM 51.)

It may surprise you to know that God is pleased if we are feeling overwhelmed and unhappy and are full of shame and despair—*if it is sin* that has brought us to that point. In fact, when we have sinned, God wants us to feel guilty. He knows that the guilt a believer feels will drive him or her to Jesus Christ and to his grace.

David was a hero of prayer—not because he sinned but because, having sinned, he found his way back to God. Many of us have heard of the story about David and Bathsheba. David's army goes out to fight while he stays behind. Passing time on the roof of his palace, he spots beautiful Bathsheba bathing on a nearby rooftop. Filled with lust, he sends for her, takes her to his bed, and she becomes pregnant. Some months later, to cover up his adultery, he conveniently arranges for her husband to be killed by the enemy in a set-up ambush.

Living a lie and having committed both adultery and murder, David feels neither guilt nor shame. But he needs to. So God sends a prophet, Nathan, who draws David emotionally into a simple story about a rich man who steals and kills the favorite lamb of a poor man to feed his guests. When David, outraged, declares that the cruel rich man in Nathan's story must die, the prophet turns the ruling back on him and says, "You are the man!" (2 Samuel 12:7).

Then David feels it. Guilt and shame! As his strength drains away and the heavy hand of God comes down on him, he cries out, "My bones [have] wasted away through all my groaning all day long" (Psalm 32:3). That's the moment God is looking for. Guilt and shame have brought David to the brink of grace. Then comes the great prayer of confession that fills the whole of Psalm 51.

True confession leads to full forgiveness, freedom from guilt and shame, and restoration of joy and gladness. When we cry out in godly sorrow, "I have sinned," that is not a groveling admission that we are terrible persons. It's the kind of confession that is full of hope and leads to a clean heart, elimination of guilt, and freedom from shame.

I used to think that confession was the most grievous and unpleasant of all the elements of prayer. From David, who found forgiveness through prayer, I have come see that it is the most satisfying, the most hopeful, and the most freeing of all prayers.

Don't let confession get you down. The truth is, real confession will lift you up like nothing else will.

Reflect

♦ Have you felt or are you feeling a sense of guilt or shame because of sin? If so, let it drive you, like David, back to God and to the cleansing he provides.

♦ Have you thought of confession as grievous and unpleasant or hopeful and freeing? What does Psalm 51 suggest?

Pray

♦ *Praise* God for his mercy. Mercy means that God does not treat us as we deserve.

♦ *Thank* God for "good guilt" that drives us into the arms of his forgiving love.

♦ *Confess* any wrong you are aware of that remains unconfessed.

♦ *Ask* for a clean heart, a renewed life, and a steadfast spirit.

♦ *Pray* that God will give his church sensitivity to sin and a readiness to confess when and if that is needed.

Act

Read Psalm 51 slowly. Use and expand on David's words, when and where they fit, as a basis for your own prayer. (See Appendix E for a "Prayers of Confession" experience.)

WEEK EIGHT

THE DIFFERENCE PRAYER MAKES

WEEK EIGHT

✸

Day One

Prayer Releases God's Power

The prayer of a righteous man is powerful and effective.
JAMES 5:16

"Prayer," said C. Samuel Storms, "in and of itself possesses no power." I was astounded by that statement, and I didn't understand it until I read what Storms said next: "Prayer is powerful because God is powerful, and prayer is the means through which that divine power is released and channeled into our lives" (*Reaching God's Ear*, p. 223). In other words, all the power in prayer is really God's power activated by prayer.

When you pray for another person, there is nothing that flows from you to them—no vibes, no force, no energy. Instead, your prayers go heavenward, and the power of God moves from him to the ones you pray for.

When the Bible says "prayer . . . is powerful and effective," it means God acts powerfully and effectively through the prayers of his people. Prayer is the instrument by which God has chosen to have his power directed in the universe. Ole Hallesby provides something of a mental picture of how this works: "This power is so rich and so mobile that all we have to do when we pray is to point to the persons or things to which we desire to have this power applied, and He, the Lord of this power, will direct the necessary power to the desired place" (*Prayer*, p. 63). What a surprising arrangement—God partnering with human beings to accomplish his purposes!

R. A. Torrey, enthralled by the enormity of this power, states, "Prayer is the key that unlocks all the storehouses of God's infinite grace and power. All that God is, and . . . has, is at the disposal of prayer. Prayer can do anything that God can do, and as God can do anything, prayer is omnipotent" (*The Power of Prayer*, p. 17).

Prayer can do what political action cannot, what education cannot, what military might cannot, and what planning committees cannot. All these are impotent by comparison.

Prayer can move mountains. It can change human hearts, families, neighborhoods, cities, and nations. It's the ultimate source of power, because it is the power of Almighty God.

This power is available to the humblest Christian. It was "a man just like us" who prayed "that it would not rain," and God stopped the rain in Israel for three and a half years. Where will the power of your prayers be felt today?

Reflect

- ◆ Where do you think God would like some of his power directed through your prayers today?
- ◆ What do you think God would like to do in your neighborhood or workplace in response to prayer?

Pray

- ◆ *Praise* God for the great power by which he moves in our world and governs the affairs of all people.
- ◆ *Thank* God for his willingness to hear our prayers and to direct his power to places and persons through them.
- ◆ *Confess* if you have failed to make use of this great privilege to advance God's cause in this world through prayer.
- ◆ *Ask* God to help you become a powerful and effective pray-er in the future.
- ◆ *Intercede* for those who live or work near you, releasing God's power and grace into their lives.

Act

As you intercede for others today, give yourself a mental picture of your prayers going heavenward to God's throne and of God directing his grace and power on earth to the very persons you are praying for.

※

Day Two

The Key to Great Works

[12]"I tell you the truth, anyone who has faith in me will do what I have been doing. He will do even greater things than these, because I am going to the Father. [13]And I will do whatever you ask in my name, so that the Son may bring glory to the Father."
JOHN 14:12-13

Jesus spoke these words shortly before he was arrested and crucified. He had just told his disciples he would be leaving them. This news left them confused and fearful—confused about the future of their work the Lord and fearful that they would not be able to do it.

Jesus' words were intended to allay the disciples' fears. He assured them that they *would be able* to do the work. In fact, they would do what he had been doing—and even greater things.

On the face of it this seems a preposterous thing for Jesus to say. After all, he had preached great sermons, attracted huge crowds, spoken wonderful words of wisdom, walked on water, stilled a storm, healed the sick, and raised the dead. How could the disciples possibly do such things?

Jesus explains that it would be possible because he was going to the Father and they would be able to ask in his name for what they needed in order to do the work of God's kingdom.

Jesus' *going* to the Father meant that he would be given all power in heaven and on earth. Thus empowered, he would continue his work on earth in a different way—through them.

Their *asking* in his name would link him to them. By means of prayer his power would be at their disposal as they carried on his ministry "to the ends of the earth" (Acts 1:8). Prayer would be "the talking part" of this ministry partnership in which he would supply the power and they would do the work.

These words of Jesus, though meant to comfort and encourage his first disciples, were also meant for us. Jesus, you will notice, addressed these surprising words to "anyone who has faith in me." That includes you, if you are a Christian, and me.

What a powerful combination: Christ on the throne of the universe, empowering us, his disciples, here on earth to build his kingdom. We ask, and he acts, and the work gets done—great works to the glory of God the Father.

What's Jesus doing through you today?

Reflect

- ◆ Have most of your prayers been for things that build the kingdom of God, or have they been somewhat more selfish?
- ◆ What things might the ascended Christ want to accomplish through you?
- ◆ Is there some place where you see great things happening in the body of Christ today?

Pray

- ◆ *Praise* Christ for the mighty works he did while he was personally on earth and for the mighty works he has accomplished through his disciples since that time.
- ◆ *Confess* if you find that your prayers have been selfishly motivated and not ministry oriented.
- ◆ *Thank* God that he is ready to hear and answer the prayers that you pray in Jesus' name.
- ◆ *Intercede* for your neighbors and coworkers using the pattern of the Lord's Prayer.

Act

Make a short list of ministries that the ascended Christ might want you to engage in that will bring glory to the Father. Tell the Lord you are willing to do whatever he asks. Do what he calls you to do in prayerful reliance on him.

✳

Day Three

The Strength to Stand

Pray in the Spirit on all occasions with all kinds of prayers and requests. With this in mind, be alert and always keep on praying for all the saints.
EPHESIANS 6:18
(READ EPHESIANS 6:10-20 AS BACKGROUND.)

God has given us prayer so that we may help each other stand. The devil is always scheming to cause us to fall. But God provides ways to help us stand victorious over the powers of evil.

Paul warns us in Ephesians 6 against the devil's schemes and the "powers of this dark world" that are constantly opposing us. Four times he uses the word "stand" to encourage us to hold out against the onslaughts of the "spiritual forces of evil" (Ephesians 6:11-14).

Standing our ground requires that we first "put on the full armor of God." We are protected against the devil by knowing the truth, being righteous, having the gospel of peace, trusting God, possessing salvation, and using the word of God in the right way. But Paul's order to "put on the full armor" does not end with "take . . . the sword of the Spirit, which is the word of God." It goes on without a break to say, "Pray in the Spirit on all occasions." In other words, the prayer support we give each other is an important part of our defense against the devil.

The prayer support required is all embracing. It's "on *all* occasions," of "*all* kinds," "*always*," and "for *all* the saints." Imagine being in the midst of a fellowship of Christians who prayed for each other this way. The possibility of falling would surely be minimized.

Several years ago God led four other men and me to start a support group and to meet together every week for an hour and a half. We covenanted to share our lives with each other as fully as possible, study the

Word of God faithfully, pursue God-given spiritual goals, and support each other in our daily prayers. What happened in the following months surprised us all. The first surprise was that almost every week one of us needed special prayer support to face a troublesome situation. Second, we all experienced spiritual growth of a kind that had eluded us in years past. And, third, every member of the group was launched into a key ministry position in the church or denomination within the next two years. As we stood together and supported each other in our daily prayers, God gave us the strength to stand and win victories.

God intends that *all* believers be strengthened to stand, as *all* take seriously the responsibility to *always* keep on praying, on *all* occasions, with *all* kinds of prayer for each other.

That's a tall order. It goes far beyond the kind of casual praying that most Christians are accustomed to. But those who pray "in the Spirit" can do it.

Reflect

♦ Do you sense that you are getting the kind of prayer support you need in order to stand?

♦ Are you giving the believers around you the kind of prayer support they need in order to stand?

♦ Is there anything more you should be doing to support the people around you in prayer? Be as specific as possible.

Pray

♦ *Thank* God for his good and wise plan to supply prayer support for every member of his body. *Thank* him for people who have given you prayer support in the past—parents, grandparents, pastors, teachers, elders in the church, and many others.

♦ If you failed to provide prayer support for those who needed your prayers, *confess* that failure to God.

♦ *Ask* God to help the community of believers you are a part of to live up to the standard of Ephesians 6:18.

♦ *Commit* yourself to serious prayer support for the people around you.

Act

Make a mental list of the believers you know who need prayer support right now. Think about pastors, teachers, evangelists, missionaries, national religious leaders, Christians in other positions of leadership, and Christians in the media, as well as those in your church community. Provide them the prayer support they need.

✻

Day Four

Prayer Defeats Satan

*³¹"Simon, Simon, Satan has asked to sift you as wheat. ³²But I
have prayed for you, Simon, that your faith may not fail. And
when you have turned back, strengthen your brothers."*
LUKE 22:31-32

There are two powerful forces at work in the world today—the power of God and the power of Satan. The power of God is infinitely greater, but we are affected by both.

Satan, bent on our destruction, goes about "like a roaring lion looking for someone to devour" (1 Peter 5:8). God, intent on our salvation, supplies "everything we need for life and godliness" (2 Peter 1:3).

Since Satan's power is greater than ours, we are constantly at risk. Paul reminds us that we struggle "against the rulers, against the authorities, against the powers of this dark world and against the spiritual forces of evil" (Ephesians 6:12). But since God's power is greater than Satan's, we are safe in God's hands. God is our constant source of protection.

Prayer is the God-given means by which God's power is brought to our defense so that we can stand up against the devil's schemes. When Peter was being severely tested by Satan, Jesus came to his defense with prayer. He said, "I have prayed for you, Simon, that your faith may not fail."

We are engaged in a war that we must fight on our knees. Prayer is the power by which we are equipped to overcome the devil. To face him in our own strength is folly and a sure pathway to defeat.

The devil dreads our prayers more than anything else. A mighty prayer warrior once said, "Do you realize that there is nothing the devil dreads so much as prayer? His great concern is to keep us from praying. He loves to see us 'up to our eyes' in work—provided we do not pray. He does not fear if we are eager Bible students—provided we are little in prayer.

Someone has wisely said, 'Satan laughs at our toiling, mocks at our wisdom, but trembles when we pray'" (*The Kneeling Christian*, p. 17).

It's no wonder that Satan trembles. By means of prayer the power of the omnipotent God of heaven and earth is brought against him. He doesn't stand a chance.

By prayer the kingdom of God is built, and by prayer the kingdom of Satan is destroyed. Where there is no prayer, there are no great works and there is no building of the kingdom. Pray much so that God may be glorified and his kingdom may come in all its fullness.

Reflect

♦ To what extent are you conscious that your prayers bring defeat to Satan's efforts?

♦ Who among your acquaintances is now being tested by Satan and is in need of your prayers?

Pray

♦ *Praise* the omnipotent God, who is able to destroy the works of the devil and protect his children.

♦ *Ask* Christ to teach you how to make use of prayer as a weapon to defeat Satan and to help advance God's kingdom.

♦ *Commit* yourself to prayerfully support the people around you, especially those whom you sense are under attack.

♦ *Pray* for those who live or work near you, asking that God will set them free from the powers of evil.

Act

Read the newspaper and watch or listen to the daily news while asking, "Is the devil involved in this tragedy, this trial, this problem?" If the answer is yes, then stand against the devil in prayer.

✳

Day Five

Prayer Shapes History

³Another angel, who had a golden censer, came and stood at the altar. He was given much incense to offer, with the prayers of all the saints, on the golden altar before the throne. ⁴The smoke of the incense, together with the prayers of the saints, went up before God from the angel's hand. ⁵Then the angel took the censer, filled it with fire from the altar, and hurled it on the earth; and there came peals of thunder, rumblings, flashes of lightning and an earthquake.
REVELATION 8:3-5

Do you get the picture here? The prayers of saints, accumulated throughout the ages on the altar of prayer, await the day when God acts on them. The day finally comes when they are brought out and answered. Hurled upon the earth, they bring about cataclysmic changes that mark the beginnings of the end of history.

Can you find yourself in the picture? You can if you have ever prayed for the coming of Christ, or if you have ever prayed that wrongs will someday be made right. Your prayers, with those of billions of other believers, will one day be answered when God brings an end to the world and establishes his glorious kingdom.

God's memory is perfect. He never forgets a prayer. Have you ever noticed that God sometimes answers prayers long after you have stopped praying them? God takes every prayer, prayed in the name of his Son, seriously—even those that were prayed centuries ago.

Today, according to statistician David Barret, there are approximately 170 million believers praying for the revival of the church and world evangelization. There are 10 million small groups praying weekly for spiritual awakening and for the completion of the Great Commission. God has heard every one of these prayers and will answer them all according to his promise and his purpose. What a day that will be!

The prayers of the saints shape history. History was shaped when Moses, from a hillside, lifted up his hands in intercession over a battlefield (Exodus 17:8-13). History was shaped when Elijah prayed "that it would not rain," and it did not rain for three and a half years in Israel (James 5:16). History was shaped when early Christians prayed until the wee hours of the morning and Peter miraculously escaped from prison (Acts 12:1-17).

In a very real sense the future of the world is in the hands of praying Christians. So is the future of your neighborhood and the future of your church, if you are a praying Christian. I hope and pray that your prayers will contribute to a glorious future for the kingdom of God right where you live—and to a still more glorious future in days to come.

Reflect
- Do you dare to believe that the lives of loved ones you pray for are being shaped through your prayers?
- How about the history of your church? Your neighborhood? Your nation? How much are your prayers contributing to the work of God in them?

Pray
- *Praise* God as the ruler of the nations, the One ultimately in charge of history.
- *Thank* God for hearing your prayers and answering them when the time is right.
- *Ask* God's forgiveness if your prayers have been so weak as to contribute almost nothing to the shaping of history.
- *Commit* yourself to faithful, fervent prayer.
- *Pray* that, in bringing history to an end, "the Sovereign Lord will wipe away the tears from all faces . . . and remove the disgrace of his people from all the earth" (Isaiah 25:8).

Act
In days and weeks to come, place on the altar of heaven many prayers for peace and justice in the world and for the swift return of Christ.

LOVE TO PRAY

GUIDE FOR
GROUP STUDY

To the Group Leader

Group leaders are encouraged to prepare by reviewing the leader notes in the back of this book prior to each meeting. Before each session the leader should

- ◆ view the video and make sure it is cued for viewing during the session.
- ◆ review the session questions and check out Bible references in the leader notes that point to answers.
- ◆ give opportunity in advance to group members who may be willing to lead in prayer.
- ◆ review and "get comfortable with" closing prayer time suggestions.

During the session the leader should

- ◆ invite brief after-the-fact reports on group members' personal prayer exercises during the previous week.
- ◆ read the questions for discussion and invite responses.
- ◆ invite someone to read the Bible passages to be studied.
- ◆ pace the discussion so that each segment gets enough time.
- ◆ involve as many group members as possible in discussion and prayer.
- ◆ suggest dividing into small groups for closing prayer times if the group is large.
- ◆ underscore the value of the personal prayer suggestions for each week.

ACTS
Adoration
Confession
Thanksgiving
Supplication

✳

WEEK ONE

What's the Good of Prayer?

In this session we will learn
- ◆ that prayer is about a love relationship with God.
- ◆ that all the elements of prayer are elements of relationship.
- ◆ that true prayer starts and ends with God.
- ◆ that the Father, the Son, and the Holy Spirit are all involved when we pray.

DVD PRESENTATION   (18 MINUTES)

What's the Good of Prayer?
Alvin VanderGriend
Prayer Evangelism Associate for Harvest Prayer Ministries

OUTLINE	NOTES
Prayer is the conversational part of the most important love relationship in our lives—our relationship with the Father, the Son, and the Holy Spirit.	
The basic elements of prayer are all components of our love relationship with God.	
Prayer definitions of others:	
True, whole prayer is nothing but love. —ST. AUGUSTINE	
Prayer is nothing more than an ongoing and growing love relationship with God the Father, Son, and Holy Spirit...To be effective pray-ers, we need to be effective lovers. —RICHARD FOSTER	

All three persons of the Trinity are involved when we pray.

Romans 8:26-27 suggests that prayer is a cycle:

> *In the same way, the Spirit helps us in our weakness. We do not know what we ought to pray for, but the Spirit himself intercedes for us with groans [yearnings] that words cannot express. And he who searches our hearts [Jesus Christ] knows the mind of the Spirit, because the Spirit intercedes for the saints in accordance with God's will.*

Loving to pray is all about loving the One to whom we pray.

The most important thing we can do to improve our prayer lives is to get to know God better.

Practical Suggestions

- Always start your prayers by asking the Holy Spirit to teach you what and how to pray.

- As you begin to pray, pause in order to consciously recall that the Father, the Son, and the Holy Spirit want what's best for you

---

Group Interaction   (10-15 minutes)

React
What insights from the presentation will make the most difference in your prayer life?

Share
Which person of the Trinity do you usually address in prayer? How do you usually think of God when you pray? (Fatherly? Gracious? Powerful? Wise? Loving?) Explain.

Discuss

Prayer is often directed *to* the Father, *through* the Son, and *by* the Holy Spirit. Why should we pray *through* the Son? Why can we pray *by* the Holy Spirit? Can we also pray *to* Son? *To* the Holy Spirit?

BIBLE STUDY   (10-15 MINUTES)

Read the following passage aloud.

> *The Spirit helps us in our weakness. We do not know what we ought to pray for, but the Spirit himself intercedes for us with groans that words cannot express. And he who searches our hearts knows the mind of the Spirit, because the Spirit intercedes for the saints in accordance with God's will.*
> —ROMANS 8:26-27

---

1. Do Paul's words in this passage suggest that we always need help to pray, or do we need help only occasionally when we might find prayer difficult? Explain.

2. The Holy Spirit's intercession is not done "for us" while we stand idly by. Rather, the Spirit intercedes for us by moving in us and through us. What prayer thoughts do you think the Spirit is bringing to life in you?

3. Revelation 2:23 identifies Jesus, the Son, as the one "who searches hearts and minds." With that in mind, describe in your own words the prayer role described in Romans 8:26-27 for each person of the Trinity. What is the prayer role of the believer?

4. When Christ searches the hearts of Christians who are praying "in the Spirit," what do you think he finds?

5. How does prayer contribute to the accomplishment of God's will on earth?

CLOSING PRAYER TIME   (10 MINUTES)

◆ Prepare for this prayer time by completing the following sentence in several different ways.
  I love you, Lord, because...

◆ Take a few moments together to express your love to God in one-sentence prayers. Start each prayer with "I love you, Lord, because..." and complete the sentence with words you have written.

◆ End by singing one or more love songs to God as a group—for example, "Father, I Adore You," "My Jesus, I Love You," or "I Love You, Lord."

PERSONAL PRAYER THIS WEEK

Prayer is often thought of as *to* the Father, *through* the Son, and *by* the Holy Spirit. Try to be conscious of and speak to the Father, the Son, and the Holy Spirit in some way every time you pray this week.

SUGGESTED READING THIS WEEK

Read the five Week One devotions in *Love to Pray* (pp. 12-21).

SPEAKER CONTACT INFORMATION

For books on prayer by Alvin VanderGriend contact
PrayerShop Publishers at 1-800-217-5200;
info@lovetopray.com or www.prayershop.org.
For seminars on prayer contact Alvin@harvestprayer.com.

WEEK TWO

The Requirements of Prayer

In this session we will learn
- ◆ that there are biblical requirements for effective prayer.
- ◆ that sin hinders prayer and prayer hinders sin.
- ◆ that confession of sin is a process with several important steps.

DVD PRESENTATION   (17 MINUTES)

The Requirements of Prayer
Paul Cedar
Director of the Mission America Coalition

OUTLINE	NOTES

The Necessity of a Clean Heart

I cried out to him with my mouth; his praise was on my tongue. If I had cherished sin in my heart, the Lord would not have listened.
—PSALM 66:17-18

If we confess our sins, he is faithful and just and will forgive us our sins and purify us from all unrighteousness. —1 JOHN 1:9

The Faith that Receives

"Have faith in God... Whatever you ask for in prayer, believe that you have received it, and it will be yours."   —MARK 11:22

The Life that Can Pray

Dear friends, if our hearts do not condemn us, we have confidence before God and receive from him anything we ask, because we obey his commands and do what pleases him. —1 JOHN 3:21-22

Praying in the Name of Jesus

"I have told you these things, so that in me you may have peace... Until now you have not asked for anything in my name. Ask and you will receive, and your joy will be complete." —JOHN 16:33, 24

Praying with Persistence

Prayer is an investment for eternity.

GROUP INTERACTION   (10-15 MINUTES)

React
Which of the biblical requirements for prayer is the hardest for you to live up to?

Share
Was there a time in your life when prayer was stronger than usual? Weaker than usual? Share one or more such experiences with your group.

Discuss
Why does sin hinder prayer? Does communal sin (such as disunity in a church) hinder communal prayer? Do you think that prayer also hinders sin? If so, why?

BIBLE STUDY   (10-15 MINUTES)

Read the following passage aloud. Let the questions direct your study.

> *"If my people, who are called by my name, will humble themselves and pray and seek my face and turn from their wicked ways, then I will hear from heaven and will forgive their sin and heal their land. Now my eyes will be open and my ears attentive to the prayers offered in this place [the temple built by Solomon in Jerusalem]."*
>   —2 CHRONICLES 7:14-15

1. In this passage what do we learn about believers? About God?

2. What does God require of believers here?

3. What does God promise to do? What does the promise "I will ...heal their land" say to Christians today?

4. In what place are the Lord's eyes open and his ears attentive to prayers today, since Solomon's temple no longer exists in Jerusalem? (See 2 Chron. 36:15-19; 1 Cor. 3:16-17; 6:19.)

5. How might things change in the church today if we really obey God and believe this promise?

CLOSING PRAYER TIME   (A PERSONAL ASSIGNMENT)

Personally review the "Prayers of Confession" in Appendix E at the back of this book. Mark any that apply to you. Then

- ◆ acknowledge that your sins grieve God's heart.
- ◆ confess them one by one to the Lord.
- ◆ ask for your Father's forgiveness.
- ◆ consciously accept God's forgiveness.
- ◆ count yourself cleansed from all unrighteousness.
- ◆ thank the Lord for his gracious forgiveness and the cleansing of the Holy Spirit.
- ◆ make a commitment to replace whatever was wrong with attitudes and actions that are right. Right(eous) acts are often directly opposite to sinful deeds.

PERSONAL PRAYER THIS WEEK

Spend personal time meeting with God in prayer each day in the coming week. Start each prayer time with quiet moments of meditation. Remember that God is alive and listening and is eager to hear from you. Imagine God's eye on you and God's ear attentive to you. Ask the Holy Spirit to give you prayer thoughts and words. Then, conscious of God's attention and the help of the Holy Spirit, pray.

SUGGESTED READING THIS WEEK

Read the five Week Two devotions in *Love to Pray* (pp. 23-33).

SPEAKER CONTACT INFORMATION

To learn more about the national ministries led by Paul Cedar, contact the Mission America Coalition at 1-760-200-2707 or www.missionamerica.org.

WEEK THREE

Claiming God's Riches

In this session we will learn
- ◆ that praying for ourselves is both necessary and fruitful.
- ◆ why we always get what we ask for when we ask in accord with God's will.
- ◆ that God always has good reasons when he says "no" to our prayers.

DVD PRESENTATION   (16 MINUTES)

Claiming God's Riches
Alvin VanderGriend
Prayer Evangelism Associate for Harvest Prayer Ministries

OUTLINE	NOTES
God wants us to ask for ourselves (petition).	
In fact, we must ask in order to receive what we need for life an d godliness (Matt. 7:11; James 4:2)	
God especially wants us to ask for "good things" (Luke 11:11-13).	
We get what we ask for when we ask according to God's will (1 John 5:14-15).	
We must ask in faith (James 1:6).	
We must ask with clean hearts and obedient spirits (1 John 3:22).	
We must ask with right motives (James 4:3).	

116

When we don't know God's will, we trust that God, in his love and wisdom, will know and do what is best (Rom. 8:28).

_____

_____

_____

_____

PRACTICAL SUGGESTIONS

◆ Memorize 1 John 5:14-15 and claim the promise in it every time you pray for yourself.

◆ Make a list of spiritual blessings that are in line with God's will and pray for them daily.

◆ Thank God for the blessings you ask for before you leave your prayer place, knowing that you will receive them.

GROUP INTERACTION   (10-15 MINUTES)

React
Which idea presented in the DVD is most important to you?

Share
Circle one intangible spiritual blessing from the following list that has meant a great deal to you:

- wisdom
- strength
- peace
- prayer
- spiritual guidance
- patience

- knowledge of God
- joy
- forgiveness
- Scripture
- hope
- filling of the Spirit

Share with the group what you have chosen and why.

Discuss
1. How can God make an absolute promise to give us what we ask if we ask in accord with his will?

2. How can we be sure that we are praying in accord with God's will?

3. Does God withhold blessings if we don't ask? Why or why not?

117

BIBLE STUDY

Read the following passage aloud. Let the questions direct your study.

> *"Which of you, if his son asks for bread, will give him a stone? Or if he asks for a fish, will give him a snake? If you, then, though you are evil, know how to give good gifts to your children, how much more will your Father in heaven give good gifts to those who ask him!"*
>
> —MATTHEW 7:9-11

---

1. What good things has God given you through your parents?

2. What good gifts would you give to your family members or friends if you could?

3. What do you know about God that makes this promise ring true?

4. Do you think it's true that God is more eager to give than we are to ask? Explain. Why aren't we more eager to ask?

CLOSING PRAYER TIME   (10 MINUTES)

Pray together in your group, each person asking for the spiritual blessings you value most. Remember that your heavenly Father is eager to give spiritual blessings to you and is pleased that you are asking. Give thanks for the gifts you will receive.

PERSONAL PRAYER THIS WEEK

Start a "gifts that God wants to give me" list. (See Appendix F) Ask for these gifts every day. Pray with the confidence that God will give you these gifts if your heart is right toward him. Thank God for them immediately. Add to this list as the Spirit leads you.

SUGGESTED READING THIS WEEK

Read the five Week Three devotions in *Love to Pray* (pp. 36-45).

SPEAKER CONTACT INFORMATION

For books on prayer by Alvin VanderGriend contact
PrayerShop Publishers at 1-800-217-5200;
info@lovetopray.com or www.prayershop.org.
For seminars on prayer contact Alvin@harvestprayer.com.

✴

WEEK FOUR

Praying for Others

In this session we will learn
- ◆ what intercessory prayer is.
- ◆ why God seeks intercessors.
- ◆ how to be powerful intercessors for those around us.

DVD Presentation   (18 minutes)

Praying for Others
Fern Nichols
Founder and Director of Moms In Touch International

OUTLINE	NOTES

We have a Mandate:
*I urge, then, first of all, that re-
quests, prayers, intercession
and thanksgiving be made for
everyone.* —1 Timothy 2:1

What Is Intercession?
Prayer for others

Biblical Examples
Abraham and Lot
Moses and the children of Israel
Jesus' intercession for Peter

Characteristics of the Intercessor
Persistent and bold (Luke 11:1-8)
Knows prayer matters to God
Knows God hears
Knows the power of prayer is in God
Knows God's heart

Examples of Powerful Intercession
Friends of a paralytic
Intercession for a prodigal

Intercession Is Ministry
Closing

*God blesses the world through our
prayer. Prayers enable us to touch
God's throne with one hand, the
needy world with the other!"*
—WESLEY DUEWEL

PRACTICAL SUGGESTIONS

◆ Start—begin now—it's never too late to pray for others. Obey the
command of 1 Timothy 2:1. It's not the great prayers we pray; it's
the great God who hears them. Don't give up. Keep praying until
God answers.

◆ Pray with friends of like passion. Burdens shared in prayer become
lighter. Hearing others pray increases your faith. Prayers multi-
plied bring about greater effect.

GROUP INTERACTION   (10-15 MINUTES)

React
What's the most important thing you learned about prayer from the
DVD presentation?

Share
In your small group, share with one another about a time when God
heard and answered your prayer for someone else.

Discuss
If God is sovereign and able to work without our prayers, why do you
think God ordinarily chooses to work through our prayers?

BIBLE STUDY (10-15 MINUTES)

Read the following passage aloud. Let the questions direct your study.

[Jesus] said to them, "Suppose one of you has a friend, and he goes to him at midnight and says, 'Friend, lend me three loaves of bread, because a friend of mine on a journey has come to me, and I have nothing to set before him.'

"Then the one inside answers, 'Don't bother me. The door is already locked, and my children are with me in bed. I can't get up and give you anything.' I tell you, though he will not get up and give him the bread because he is his friend, yet because of the man's boldness he will get up and give him as much as he needs." —LUKE 11:5-8

---

1. If in this parable the friend-with-bread represents God, who does the friend-in-need represent? Who does the friend-in-the-middle represent?

2. How would you describe the "prayer" of the friend-in-the-middle?

3. What does this passage say to us about awareness of need? Who in your personal life right now might be a friend-in-need?

4. What does this passage say to us about praying for others?

Closing Prayer Time   (10 minutes)

Each person in your small group should mention briefly the name and situation of one person known to be a friend-in-need. Then, one by one, group members can pray for each person named.

Personal Prayer This Week

Make a list of persons for whom God would have you intercede on a regular basis. Start with family and friends, but ask God to remind you of certain coworkers, classmates, neighbors, and acquaintances as well. Keep the list in a prominent place, and pray for these persons regularly.

Suggested Reading This Week

Read the five Week Four devotions in *Love to Pray* (pp. 48-57).

Speaker Contact Information

To learn how to start a Moms In Touch group or to receive information on Fern Nichols' books contact Moms In Touch 1-800-949-6667; info@momsintouch.org or www.momsintouch.org.

WEEK FIVE

Prayer as a Way of Life

In this session we will learn
- ◆ that we can and should learn to "pray without ceasing."
- ◆ how to share thoughts, feelings, and experiences with God all the time.
- ◆ that we can and should listen to God as well as talk to God.

DVD PRESENTATION   (17 MINUTES)
Prayer as a Way of Life
David Butts
Director of Harvest Prayer Ministries
Chairman of the National Prayer Committee

OUTLINE	NOTES
We have a tendency to compart-mentalize life.	

Scripture teaches that prayer is a way of life.

Jesus told his disciples a parable to show them that they should always pray... —LUKE 18:1

Pray continually.
            —1 THESSALONIANS 5:17

Pray in the Spirit on all occasions with all kinds of prayers and requests. With this in mind, be alert and always keep on praying for all the saints.
—EPHESIANS 6:18

Prayer is who we are.

We are "houses of prayer". God's glory dwells in us.

> *"My house will be called a house of prayer for all nations."*
> —ISAIAH 56:7

Jesus was a "house of prayer."

> *"I do nothing on my own but speak just what the Father has taught me."* —JOHN 8:28

How to make prayer a way of life

Be aware that Christ lives in us.

...Christ in you, the hope of glory.
—COLOSSIANS 1:27

Narrow the gaps of unawareness.

Set up flags of awareness throughout the day.

_____
_____
_____
_____
_____
_____
_____
_____
_____
_____
_____
_____
_____
_____
_____
_____

GROUP INTERACTION   (10-15 MINUTES)

React
What did you learn about prayer from the DVD presentation?

Share
Most believers habitually think to pray at certain times—for example, at meal times, when they get up in the morning, before bedtime, when they start a meeting, and so on. Share with the group some times or situations when you ordinarily think to pray.

Discuss
1. Is it better to talk to God in everyday words and phrases, or should we try to use more formal language with God? Explain.

2. If we are doing something that we know is wrong, should we try to talk to God at that moment or should we wait and try to clear things up with God later? Explain.

BIBLE STUDY   (10-15 MINUTES)

Read the following passage aloud. Let the questions direct your study.
*Pray in the Spirit on all occasions with all kinds of prayers and re-
quests. With this in mind, be alert and always keep on praying for all
the saints.*   —EPHESIANS 6:18

---

1. In what ways is the Spirit able to help us in our praying?

2. Identify the three "alls" in this verse and note a fourth all that means
   "all the time." Describe in your own words the standard for prayer to
   which this passage holds us.

3. What "occasions," common or uncommon, would give rise to a
   prayer of praise? A prayer of thanks? Of confession? Of petition? Of
   intercession?

4. What does the writer have in mind by asking us to pray "all kinds of
   prayers and requests"?

5. In light of earlier remarks in Ephesians 6 about struggling "against
   the spiritual forces of evil" (6:12), why is being alert and "praying for
   all the saints" so important?

CLOSING PRAYER TIME   (A PERSONAL ASSIGNMENT)

Ephesians 6:18 reminds us to "always keep on praying for all the saints." That would include

- believers who are being persecuted for their faith.
- believers in key government positions.
- pastors, most of whom bear heavy loads.
- believers who work in media industries.
- parents who find it difficult to bring up children in a secular society.
- new believers who are being tested by powers of darkness.
- believers who are experiencing marital difficulties.
- young believers on secular college campuses.

Add some examples of your own to the above list and then spend time in your small group praying for believers who struggle "against the spiritual forces of evil."

PERSONAL PRAYER THIS WEEK

At the beginning of each day this week, ask God to help you be conscious of him again and again throughout the day Respond to God each time you think of him. Remember, your response could be praise, confession, thanksgiving, petition, or intercession. End your response with a prayer asking God to help you be conscious of him again soon.

SUGGESTED READING THIS WEEK

Read the five Week Five devotions in *Love to Pray* (pp. 60-69).

SPEAKER CONTACT INFORMATION

To learn more about David Butt's books and ministries contact
1-800-217-5200; info@harvestprayer.com or www.prayershop.org.

✳

WEEK SIX

Model Prayers of the Bible

In this session we will learn

◆ that the emphasis in model prayers from the New Testament is
   clearly on spiritual blessings.
◆ that the burden of our intercessory prayers should be to propel
   others onward and upward in their spiritual journeys.
◆ that our confidence when praying is not in prayer but in the
   One to whom we pray.

DVD PRESENTATION   (16 MINUTES)

Model Prayers of the Bible
Jarvis Ward
Facilitator of City-Community Ministries
for the Mission America Coalition

OUTLINE	NOTES
Why are prayers recorded in the Bible?	
God wants us to know him.	
Models inform our prayers.	
We see how others related to him.	
They enrich our relationship with God.	
Model prayers from the Old Testament	
Isaiah 25:1—adoration, praise, and worship	
O Lord, thou art my God; I will exalt thee, I will praise thy name; for thou hast done wonderful	

things; thy counsels of old are faithfulness and truth. (RSV)

Daniel 9:4-6—confession

Daniel 2:23—thanksgiving and praise

Model prayers from the New Testament

Matthew 6:9-13—the Lord's Prayer is a model of Scripture praying.

Ephesians 1:16-20—knowing Christ better

Ephesians 3:14-17—Christ at home in our hearts

Colossians 1:9-13—a good way to intercede for others

PRACTICAL SUGGESTIONS

◆ Use Colossians 1:9-13 as a model to pray spiritual blessings on others.

◆ Pray an expanded version of the Lord's Prayer.

GROUP INTERACTION   (10-15 MINUTES)

React
What interested you most in the DVD presentation?

Share
Share with each other how you learned to pray. Were you taught to pray memorized prayers? Did these prayers help you build a relationship with God, or did they reinforce ritualistic prayer?

Discuss
Would you agree or disagree with this statement: "Prayer should rise more out of God's Word and concern for his kingdom than even out of our own personal needs, trials, or desires"? Why? What are the practical implications of your position?

BIBLE STUDY   (10-15 MINUTES)

Read the following passage aloud. Let the questions direct your study.

> *Since the day we heard about you, we have not stopped praying for you and asking God to fill you with the knowledge of his will through all spiritual wisdom and understanding. And we pray this in order that you may live a life worthy of the Lord and may please him in every way: bearing fruit in every good work, growing in the knowledge of God, being strengthened with all power according to his glorious might so that you may have great endurance and patience, and joyfully giving thanks to the Father, who has qualified you to share in the inheritance of the saints in the kingdom of light.*
> —COLOSSIANS 1:9-12

1. Which of the spiritual blessings mentioned in Colossians 1:9-12 would you most treasure?

2. Do you think it would make any difference in the lives of persons you know if you prayed this prayer regularly for them? Why or why not?

3. Would God have blessed the Colossian Christians with these spiritual blessings even if the writer, Paul, hadn't prayed this way?

4. How might Paul's prayer for the Colossians differ from the requests for prayer made in our churches? How could a church transition from offering mostly requests for personal needs and concerns to offering more prayers for "spiritual blessing"?

Closing Prayer Time   (10 minutes)

◆ Group members pray together for the spiritual well-being of family members, friends, or fellow believers in a way like Paul does in his prayer for the Colossians.

Personal Prayer This Week

Memorize Colossians 1:9-12 so that you can pray these spiritual blessings for others from memory. As you pray these prayer themes, try to expand on them and tailor them to specific persons and situations.

Suggested Reading This Week

Read the five Week Six devotions in *Love to Pray* (pp. 72-81).

Speaker Contact Information

To learn more about the City Reaching ministries led by Jarvis Ward
or to inquire about a prayer seminar contact
601-608-0046; Jarvis@cityreaching.com or www.cityreaching.com.

✸

WEEK SEVEN

Heroes of Prayer

In this session we will learn

- ◆ that Jesus Christ is our prime example of prayer.
- ◆ that the Lord's Prayer is meant to be a model for our prayers, not simply repeated by rote.
- ◆ that the Lord's Prayer contains all the DNA necessary to produce authentic spirituality.

DVD PRESENTATION   (16 MINUTES)

Heroes of Prayer
Henry Blackaby
Director of Blackaby Ministries International

OUTLINE	NOTES
The heart of prayer is to be found in the life of Jesus Christ.	
At every major moment of his life Jesus prayed.	
The Father summoned Jesus to prayer.	
Jesus always found the will of God through prayer.	
Jesus often withdrew into the wilderness and prayed.	
Jesus heard from the Father in prayer.	
Prayer is the way to know God's agenda.	
The Father orchestrated the prayer life of Jesus.	
The great confession	

Choosing the Twelve

The mount of transfiguration

Gethsemane

The cross

God's whole plan rests on our hearing, understanding, and obeying his will.

> The essence of prayer is when the Father reveals his will.

> Prayer is intimate fellowship with God.

We need to follow the model of the Lord Jesus Christ.

> Prayer was the way Jesus related to the Father.

> Does our prayer come out of a relationship with God?

Heaven's door is always open to us.

> *We have confidence to enter the Most Holy Place by the blood of Jesus, by a new and living way...*
> —Hebrews 10:19-20

Group Interaction   (10-15 minutes)

React

What impresses you most about Jesus' prayer life?

Share

What aspects of your prayer life are most like Jesus' prayer life? What aspects are least like Jesus' prayer life? What would help you become more like Jesus in your prayer life?

Discuss

If Jesus has "all authority in heaven and on earth" (Matt. 28:18), why does he continue to intercede for us (Rom. 8:34)? What does this tell us about the relationship between the Father and the Son? About the importance of intercession?

BIBLE STUDY   (10-15 MINUTES)

Read the following passage aloud. Let the questions direct your study.

"This, then, is how you should pray:

"'Our Father in heaven,
hallowed be your name,
your kingdom come,
your will be done on earth as it is in heaven.
Give us today our daily bread.
Forgive us our debts, as we also have forgiven our debtors.
And lead us not into temptation,
but deliver us from the evil one.'"

—MATTHEW 6:9-13

---

1. What does the opening phrase "our Father" tell us about who can pray this prayer and who can't?

2. What do the pronouns "our" and "us" tell us about the scope God intends our prayers to have?

3. What are the Father's three greatest concerns that need to be addressed in prayer? What are the believer's three greatest needs?

4. What does the amount of space given to God's concerns in this prayer teach us about shaping our prayers?

5. What does the sequence of these two groups of petitions teach us about priorities in our prayers?

6. Jesus—the greatest "pray-er" who ever lived—now lives in us. What are the implications of this for us and our praying?

CLOSING PRAYER TIME (A PERSONAL ASSIGNMENT)

The best way to use a model prayer is to take the core idea in each petition and to expand on it. Try to do this now in prayer as you intentionally spend time on each petition. Try to follow the order provided in the Lord's Prayer.

PERSONAL PRAYER THIS WEEK

Pray an expanded version of the Lord's Prayer daily this week, and imagine some ways in which God is responding to your petitions. Imagine God, for example, making his presence felt in a worship service (hallowing), blessing crops with rain and sunshine (giving bread), and giving Christians the strength to resist temptations.

SUGGESTED READING THIS WEEK

Read the five Week Seven devotions in *Love to Pray* (pp. 84-93).

SPEAKER CONTACT INFORMATION

To learn more about Henry Blackaby's ministries contact
Blackaby Ministries International at
404-362-9500 or speakers@blackaby.org.

✳

WEEK EIGHT

Why Prayer Makes a Difference

In this session we will learn
- ◆ that prayer is powerful because God is powerful.
- ◆ that our prayers direct God's power to particular persons or places.
- ◆ that prayer is the key factor in effective ministry.
- ◆ that the prayers of God's people shape history.

DVD PRESENTATION   (18 MINUTES)

Why Prayer Makes a Difference
Dana Olson and Alvin VanderGriend
Dana is Director of Prayer First for the General Baptist Convention
and Chairman of the Denominational Prayer Leaders' Network

OUTLINE	NOTES
Prayer is not a way to get "our" way.	
Prayer does more than simply change us.	
Prayer is where salvation begins.	
Prayer releases God's grace and power.	
Prayer gives us the strength to stand.	
Prayer makes a difference in families.	

Prayer makes a difference in churches.

_____

_____

God governs the world through the prayers of his people.

_____

_____

PRACTICAL SUGGESTIONS

♦ When you pray for others, imagine your prayers going heavenward and releasing God's power and grace directly into people's lives.

♦ Make a list of the people around you—family, friends, coworkers, neighbors—who do not appear to know Christ and his saving grace. Pray for them regularly.

GROUP INTERACTION   (10-15 MINUTES)

React
What are some things you learned about prayer from the DVD presentation?

Share
Share with group members about a time when prayer made a difference in your life or in the life of someone you prayed for.

Discuss
How would you respond to a person who said, "Everything is predestined, so prayer doesn't really make any difference"?

BIBLE STUDY   (10-15 MINUTES)

Read the following passage aloud. Let the questions direct your study.

> *"I tell you the truth, anyone who has faith in me will do what I have been doing. He will do even greater things than these, because I am going to the Father. And I will do whatever you ask in my name, so that the Son may bring glory to the Father. You may ask me for anything in my name, and I will do it."*   —JOHN 14:12-14

1. Who can lay claim to this astonishing promise?

2. What are some things Christ did while he was on earth that believers are doing today? What works today are "even greater" than the things Jesus did during his earthly ministry?

3. Where is Christ and what is he doing as we are doing these "greater things"?

4. What is the place of prayer when it comes to doing Christ's works today?

5. How must we ask in order to be sure our prayers are heard on high? Can we still do great works if we don't ask?

6. What is Christ's great objective in urging, hearing, and answering our prayers?

CLOSING PRAYER TIME   (10 MINUTES)

Praise Christ for the mighty works being accomplished on earth today because believers are praying and he is working in and through their prayers! Thank God for prayer and the difference it makes. Ask God to deepen your prayer lives and to give you spiritual works to do that will glorify his name.

PERSONAL PRAYER THIS WEEK

Ask yourself, "Where would God like some of his power directed through my prayers today?" (Think of family members, coworkers, neighbors, church, community, and more.) Ask the ascended Christ to work in all of these areas, and make yourself available to accomplish his will on earth.

SUGGESTED READING THIS WEEK

Read the five Week Eight devotions in *Love to Pray* (pp. 96-105).

SPEAKER CONTACT INFORMATION

Dana Olson can be reached at 1-800-323-4215 or bigdana@aol.com.

✳

LEADER NOTES
Week One: Leader

Prepare for the lesson by viewing the DVD, working through the following sections and doing the Week One devotions before the group study session. (Plan on preparing this way for each lesson.)

- Begin with a prayer that reflects the theme of the lesson you are about to study.
- Take some time to get acquainted.
- Ask participants what they would like to get out of this study.

DVD PRESENTATION

Before each DVD session . . .
- Cue the DVD to the right spot for the session.
- Invite group members to look at the React and Share questions and think about how they will answer after viewing the DVD.

GROUP INTERACTION

Read each question aloud to start the interaction.

Share
- How we address God will have an effect on the way we pray.

Discuss
- "through the Son"—see John 14:13 and 16:23-24.
- "by the Holy Spirit"—see Rom. 8:26-27 and 1 Cor. 2:10-13.
- "to the Son"—see John 14:14.
- "to the Holy Spirit"—think of songs addressed to the Holy Spirit.

BIBLE STUDY

QUESTIONS:
2. "Spirit moving in us"—"intercede" in the Greek language means "meets with in order to converse"
"groanings"—the Spirit's intercessory "groanings" are the Spirit's longings for the Father's will to be done.

4. "what Christ finds?"—consider all the elements of prayer, often summarized as adoration, confession, thanksgiving, supplication.

CLOSING PRAYER TIME

♦ Encourage people to pray more than one sentence prayer during the prayer time. If the group is large, split into smaller groups. Groups of 7-10 persons can make room for some to pray silently.

♦ Accompaniment is not necessary for the singing. Select a person with musical ability to start the singing.

SUGGESTED READING

Make sure everyone has access to a copy of *Love to Pray*. Encourage everyone to read the Week One devotions ("What's the Good of Prayer?") and to take enough time to work through the Reflect, Pray, and Act sections each day.

Week Two: Leader

Begin with a prayer that reflects the lesson you are about to study.

DVD PRESENTATION

Remind the group of the React and Share questions that will follow the DVD.

GROUP INTERACTION

Share

♦ The leader may go first. Doing so can establish a healthy level of transparency that others will follow.

Discuss

♦ sin hinders prayer—see Ps. 66:18; Isa. 59:1-2.
♦ prayer hinders sin—see Luke 22:32; 1 Thess. 5:23.

BIBLE STUDY

QUESTIONS: 5. See Deut. 28:1-14.

CLOSING PRAYER TIME

Give group members time to get started on the "Prayers of Confession" list and on some personal confession time. Encourage members to continue examination and confession on their own in the week following this lesson.

ALTERNATIVE CLOSING: For a different experience you could invite the group to first identify and then confess sins and failures of your church or of the general church of Christ within your nation.

PERSONAL PRAYER

Underscore the value of a personal prayer time and the suggestions given. Promise to give group members time during your next session to report on their experiences.

SUGGESTED READING

Build anticipation for the Week Two devotional readings ("The Requirements of Prayer") by connecting them with your discussion from this session.

Week Three: Leader

- Remember to give group members an opportunity to report on their personal prayer experiences of the past week.
- Have a group member open with prayer. (Make sure you give the person an opportunity to prepare in advance.)

DVD PRESENTATION

Before showing the DVD, call the group's attention to the React and Share questions that will follow the viewing.

GROUP INTERACTION

Discuss
1. See James 1:5-6; 1 John 3:22.
2. See John 15:7.
3. See James 4:2-3.

CLOSING PRAYER TIME

- If the group is large, divide into small groups.
- Participants shouldn't be embarrassed to pray for themselves in a

small group. They are actually sharing themselves with the group when they do this.

ALTERNATIVE CLOSING: Divide into triplets. Each person shares a spiritual blessing he or she would like to receive. Another person in the triplet asks God to grant this blessing.

PERSONAL PRAYER

Emphasize the value of this take-home assignment. Check out Appendix A together. Suggest a "report back" time at the beginning of your next session.

SUGGESTED READING

Stir everyone's interest in the Week Three devotional readings ("Claiming God's Riches") by highlighting one or two important insights from them.

Week Four: Leader

◆ Give group members an opportunity to report on the prayers they have prayed in the past week to claim God's riches.
◆ Prepare for this lesson on intercession by distinguishing petition (asking for ourselves) from intercession (asking on behalf of others).

DVD PRESENTATION

Note that the Moms in Touch International ministry, led by our DVD presenter, engages in a worldwide ministry of intercession for children.

GROUP INTERACTION

Discuss
◆ See Eph. 3:10; 2 Cor 1:10-11.

CLOSING PRAYER TIME

Encourage group members to include the names of persons who don't know the Lord. Salvation is the highest need.

PERSONAL PRAYER

Stress the importance of making a concrete list of unsaved or hurting persons to be prayed for. The list doesn't have to be long. Once each person has started a list, the Lord will add to it as the person is prepared to handle more.

SUGGESTED READING

Take a brief look at the BLESS acronym on page 51 of *Love to Pray* in anticipation of this week's take-home assignment.

Week Five: Leader

◆ Ask group members about their experiences with intercessory prayer lists and the BLESS prayer pattern.
◆ In your opening prayer give glory to the Father, Son, and Holy Spirit for the ways in which they are engaged in prayer, and ask for their help.

DVD PRESENTATION

As you prepare to present the DVD, invite everyone to reflect on the meaning of "Prayer as a Way of Life."

GROUP INTERACTION

Share
◆ In the gospels Jesus is reported to have prayed many times. How many of those occasions can you think of?

Discuss
1. See Jer. 29:12-13; Matt. 6:7.
2. See Eph. 4:26-27.

BIBLE STUDY

QUESTIONS:
1. See Rom. 8:26-27; 1 Cor. 2:10-13.
3. See 1 Thess. 5:17.
4. Review the ACTS acronym that includes all the basic elements of prayer—Adoration, Confession, Thanksgiving, Supplication (includes petition and intercession).
5. See Rom. 15:30-31; 2 Thess. 3:1-2.

CLOSING PRAYER TIME

This prayer can be done in a large group. To relieve the tension some people may have about when and how they might contribute, ask for volunteers to pray for certain concerns before the prayer begins.

PERSONAL PRAYER

Encourage group members to pray for each other as well as for themselves in the coming week, asking that God will help them be conscious of him throughout each day.

SUGGESTED READING

Note that the devotional reading for Day 4 of this week ("Praying the Ordinary") deals with Eph. 6:18, which you have just studied together.

Week Six: Leader

- ◆ Ask group members if they experienced a greater consciousness of God as a result of the past week's personal prayer exercise.
- ◆ In your opening prayer give thanks for increased awareness of God and practice in prayer. Ask the Holy Spirit to help all of you become better "pray-ers."

DVD PRESENTATION

Make one or two preview comments about the DVD as you begin.

GROUP INTERACTION

Discuss

- ◆ You may wish to note that the statement marked with an asterisk (*) is a quote from Donald G. Bloesch, *The Struggle of Prayer*.

BIBLE STUDY

- ◆ Col. 1:9-12 is only one of Paul's great "spiritually focused" prayers. Eph. 1:16-23, Eph. 3:14-19, and Phil. 1:9-11 are equally noteworthy.

QUESTIONS:

1. To see how God tends to act in response to prayer rather than when there is no prayer, see Ezek. 22:30-31. (Take note of Ezek. 22:23-29 as well.) Compare the Ezekiel passage to Psalm 106:23.

2. What percentage of prayer requests in your church do you think are for personal needs and concerns?

CLOSING STUDY

Some group members might want to turn to Eph. 1:16-23, Eph. 3:14-19, Phil. 1:9-11, 1 Tim. 6:11-12, or 2 Pet. 1:5-8 and pray the words of these Scriptures during this prayer time.

PERSONAL PRAYER

Mention that group members can start by praying Col. 1:9-12 for themselves. This is a prayer that's in line with God's will.

SUGGESTED READING

The devotional reading for Day Three on pages 76-77 will help expand your perspective on Col. 1:9-12.

Week Seven: Leader

- ◆ Inquire about group members' experiences with Col. 1:9-12 throughout the past week.
- ◆ Have someone lead in opening prayer. Invite everyone to focus on the "spiritual blessings" you'll be discussing during this session.

DVD PRESENTATION

Henry Blackaby is best known for his widely read book *Experiencing God*. He is the director of Blackaby Ministries International.

GROUP INTERACTION

Share

- ◆ For further study of Jesus' prayer life, see Mark 1:35; 6:46; Luke 5:16; 6:12; 9:18; Matt. 19:13; Heb. 5:7.

Discuss

- ◆ Heb. 7:25 and John 15:26 will help cast some light on this question.

SUGGESTED READING

In addition to reading the Week Seven devotions on pages 82-93, you may want to reread "Our Lord's Model Prayer" on pages 72-73.

Week Eight: Leader

GROUP INTERACTION

Discuss

♦ "Predestined" means "decided ahead of time." One thing we can be sure of is that God has decided ahead of time to answer prayer. He promised that he would (see Luke 11:9-10; John 16:24).

♦ See Ex. 17:8-13, Ps. 106:23, and Ezek. 22:30-31 on how prayer may affect moments in history.

BIBLE STUDY

QUESTIONS:

3. See Eph. 1:20-23; John 14:2-4; Rom. 8:34.

5. Asking "in Jesus' name" means asking in harmony with his will and based on his work.

SUGGESTED READING

This week you and your group will complete your reading of *Love to Pray*. Give some thought to going through the book a second time. It takes time, and often repeated attempts, to lock in good devotional habits.

LOVE TO PRAY

APPENDICES

APPENDIX A

The BLESSing Prayer

B **Body**—(pray for health, protection, strength, fitness)
"Seek first [God's] kingdom and his righteousness, and all these things will be given to you as well" (Matt. 6:33).
> Lord, may _____ seek your kingdom first and discover that food, clothing, health, and protection are given to them as well.

L **Labor**—(pray for a good job, income, financial security)
Whatever you do, work at it with all your heart, as working for the Lord, not for men, since you know that you will receive an inheritance from the Lord as a reward. It is the Lord Christ you are serving (Col. 3:23-24).
> Lord, I pray that _____ will be diligent in work with a sense that they are serving you in everything they do, aware of the inheritance (full life forever) that will come from you.

E **Emotional**—(pray for joy, peace, patience, self-control)
You will keep in perfect peace him whose mind is steadfast, because he trusts in you (Isa. 26:3).
> Lord, give _____ the ability to keep their focus on you and to always know that you are ready to meet all their needs and to give them your peace.

S **Social**—(pray for marriage, family, friends, love, forgiveness)
Be kind and compassionate to one another, forgiving each other, just as in Christ God forgave you (Eph. 4:32).
> Lord, help _____ to be as kind, compassionate, and forgiving to others as you are to them. Give them a network of supportive friends and many good relationships.

S **Spiritual**—(pray for salvation, spiritual growth, grace, hope)
Taste and see that the Lord is good; blessed is the man who takes refuge in him (Ps. 34:8).
> Lord, I pray that _____ will understand just how good you are and will take refuge in you. May they grow in the grace and knowledge of the Lord Jesus Christ.

Note: The BLESS acronym is an easy way to remember five important ways to intercede for others. Use this pattern to pray for family members, friends, neighbors, and coworkers.

APPENDIX B

Praying "With All Kinds of Prayer"

PRAISE—*Oh, the depth of the riches of the wisdom and knowledge of God! How unsearchable his judgments, and his paths beyond tracing out!* (Rom. 11:33).
I *praise* you, God, for the richness of your wisdom and knowledge, and I rejoice in your unsearchable ways. I exalt your name and . . .

THANKS—*My God will meet all your needs according to his glorious riches in Christ Jesus* (Phil. 4:19).
Thank you, God, for meeting all my needs—temporal, physical, emotional, spiritual, and eternal. I am especially grateful that . . .

CONFESSION—*"Do not worry about your life, what you will eat of drink; or about your body, what you will wear"* (Matt. 6:25).
Forgive me, Lord, for being anxious about things that are happening to me that you have completely in your control. I confess that . . .

PETITION—*"Remain in me and I will remain in you. No branch can bear fruit by itself; it must remain in the vine. Neither can you bear fruit unless you remain in me"* (John 15:4).
Help me, Lord, to live in union with you. Thank you for your readiness to live in union with me so that I can bear much fruit and be your disciple. I ask that . . .

INTERCESSION—*"All men will hate you because of me, but he who stands firm to the end will be saved"* (Matt. 10:22).
I *pray*, Lord, for persecuted Christians around the world, asking that they will be able to stand firm. In addition I pray that . . .

SUBMISSION—*Be devoted to one another in brotherly love. Honor one another above yourselves. . . . Live in harmony with one another. Do not be proud . . .* (Rom. 12:10, 16).
Lord, I *resolve* to love my fellow brothers and sisters in Christ and to honor them above myself. I will . . .

Note: Ponder each verse above with the awareness that God is telling you what he thinks. Respond back to God by telling him what you think. This is one way to pray Scripture. Try to give about the same amount of time to each element.

APPENDIX C

Prayers of Praise

Praise God who is . . .

LOVING—*How great is the love the Father has lavished on us, that we should be called children of God! And that is what we are!* (1 John 3:1).

    I praise you, Father, for your *lavish love,* and I rejoice that you have made me your child. When I think of your love, I . . .

SOVEREIGN RULER—*"Wealth and honor come from you; you are the ruler of all things. In your hands are strength and power to exalt and give strength to all"* (1 Chron. 29:12).

    I exalt you, my *God and King.* By your strength and power you touch my life and . . .

POWERFUL—*Now to him who is able to do immeasurably more than all we ask or imagine, according to his power at work within us, to him be glory in the church and in Christ Jesus throughout all generations, forever and ever!* (Eph. 3:20-21).

    I glorify you, God, for your *great power.* Use your power at work in me to . . .

GRACIOUS—*God is able to make all grace abound to you, so that in all things at all times, having all that you need, you will abound in every good work* (2 Cor. 9:8).

    I honor you, God, for your *amazing grace* at work in my heart and life. Because of your grace I know that . . .

GOOD—*Taste and see that the Lord is good; blessed is the man who takes refuge in him* (Ps. 34:8).

    I praise you, Lord, for you *goodness.* I want to taste as much of it as possible. Because of your goodness I . . .

HOLY—*[The seraphim] were calling to one another: "Holy, holy, holy is the Lord Almighty; the whole earth is full of his glory"* (Isa. 6:3).

    In harmony with the angels gathered around your throne I praise you, saying, *"Holy, holy, holy is the Lord almighty".* I see your holiness in . . .

MERCIFUL—*"Who is a God like you, who pardons sin and forgives the transgression of the remnant of his inheritance? You do not stay angry forever but delight to show mercy"* (Mic. 7:18).

    I praise you, Lord, as a *merciful* God, slow to anger and abounding in lovingkindness. I am so glad that . . .

152

APPENDIX D

Prayers of Thanksgiving

Thank God for . . .

NEEDS MET—*My God will meet all your needs according to his glorious riches in Christ Jesus* (Phil. 4:19).

Thank you, Lord, for meeting my needs—physical, emotional, and spiritual. You are so generous with your riches that I . . .

THE HOLY SPIRIT—*"If you then, though you are evil, know how to give good gifts to your children, how much more will your Father in heaven give the Holy Spirit to those who ask him!"* (Luke 11:13).

For me to have your Spirit, Father, is to have every spiritual blessing that you give—life, wisdom, power, guidance and the fruit of the Spirit. Thank you so much for . . .

STRENGTH—*"The eyes of the Lord range throughout the earth to strengthen those whose hearts are fully committed to him"* (2 Chron. 16:9).

Thank you, God, for the strength to serve. You always know how to help. I am so grateful that . . .

PRAYERS HEARD—*Know that the Lord has set apart the godly for himself; the Lord will hear when I call to him* (Ps. 4:3).

God, I am so grateful that you are always ready to hear when I pray. I can hardly believe that I am so special to you that . . .

PEACE—*"Peace I leave with you; my peace I give you. I do not give to you as the world gives. Do not let your hearts be troubled and do not be afraid"* (John 14:27).

Thank you, God, for giving me your peace. In this world of noise, anxiety, and busyness it's what I really need. With that I . . .

ETERNAL LIFE—*God has given us eternal life, and this life is in his Son. He who has the Son has life; he who does not have the Son of God does not have life* (1 John 5:11-12).

Thank you, Father, for giving me the gift of eternal life—the life that is in your Son, Jesus Christ. I've never had a better gift. Having that, I . . .

THE WORD—*All Scripture is God-breathed and is useful for teaching, rebuking, correcting and training in righteousness, so that the man of God may be thoroughly equipped for every good work* (2 Tim. 3:16-17).

Thank you, God, for giving me your Word so that I am able to know the truth about you and how to truly live. I will . . .

APPENDIX E

Prayers of Confession

Confess to God if . . .

. . . your answer to any of the following questions is "yes."

WORRY—*"Do not worry about your life, what you will eat or drink; or about your body, what you will wear"* (Matt. 6:25).

Am I worried about material things? Unduly anxious about money? Overly concerned about my appearance?

GREED—*"Do not store up for yourselves treasures on earth . . . . But store up for yourselves treasures in heaven . . . . For where your treasure is, there your heart will be also"* (Matt. 6:19-21).

Do I treasure material possessions more than spiritual riches? Is my heart tuned mainly to things? Do I own a lot of unnecessary things?

LUST—*"Anyone who looks at a woman lustfully has already committed adultery with her in his heart"* (Matt. 5:28).

Have I looked lustfully at a person, magazine, television program, or at Internet pornography? Do I think lustful thoughts and/or engage in lustful acts?

PRIDE—*Do not think of yourself more highly than you ought, but rather think of yourself with sober judgment* (Rom. 12:3).

Am I proud of my abilities, my accomplishments, my personal looks, or my bank account? Do I see others as less important, in many ways, than I am?

UNFORGIVENESS—*Bear with each other and forgive whatever grievances you may have against one another. Forgive as the Lord forgave you* (Col. 3:13).

Is there anyone whom I have not forgiven? Am I purposely avoiding someone? Holding on to a grudge? Talking to people about the offenses of others?

DISHONESTY—*Do not lie to each other, since you have taken off your old self with its practices and have put on the new self* (Col. 3:9-10).

Do I exaggerate, understate, cover my misdeeds with half-truths, or cheat others? Do I tell "white lies," thinking that's okay?

UNWHOLESOME TALK—*Do not let any unwholesome talk come out of your mouths, but only what is helpful for building others up* (Eph. 4:29).

Do I use filthy language or tell off-color jokes? Do I diminish others by what I say to them or by what I say to others about them?

APPENDIX F

Prayers of Petition

You can **petition God for** . . .

. . . any or all of the following spiritual blessings for yourself with the confidence that you will be given what you ask because they are in line with God's will (1 John 5:14-15). This assumes that you ask in faith and have a pure heart.

A—*abiding* in Christ (John 15:4-5)

B— *blessed* with every spiritual blessing in Christ (Eph. 1:3)

C—*conformed* to the likeness of Christ (Rom. 8:29)

D—*delivered* from the evil one (Matt. 6:13)

E— *equipped* for works of service (Eph. 4:11-13)

F— *forgiven* of my sins (Matt. 6:12)

G—*grace upon grace* from his fullness (John 1:16)

H—*holiness* in all I do (1 Pet. 1:16)

I— *integrity* and uprightness (Ps. 25:21)

J— *joy* of the Lord, complete in me (John 15:11)

K—*knowledge* and depth of insight (Phil. 1:9)

L— *love* for God and neighbor (Matt. 22:37-39)

M—*meditating* on the Word of God (Ps. 1:2)

N—*new mind*, new self (Eph. 4:23-24)

O—*obedience* to all that Christ commands (Matt. 28:20)

P— *prayer* in the Holy Spirit (Eph. 6:18)

Q—*quietness* and trust as your strength (Isa. 30:15)

R— *righteousness*, peace, and joy in the Spirit (Rom. 14:17)

S— *strong* in the Lord and his mighty power (Eph. 6:10)

T—*thinking* God-honoring thoughts (Phil. 4:8)

U—*useful* to the master (2 Tim. 2:21; 1 Pet. 4:10)

V—*virtues* covered with love (Col. 3:14)

W—*worship* in spirit and in truth (John 4:24)

X—*X-rayed* by the Spirit (Ps. 139:23-24)

Y—*yearning* for God (Ps. 84:2; Isa. 26:9)

Z— *zeal* in the service of the Lord (Rom. 12:11)

APPENDIX G

Prayers of Submission

Submit to God . . .

Try to say a sincere "yes" to each of these commands of God and to the critique questions that follow each verse. Plan practical ways to live out your "yes."

LOVE—*Love must be sincere. Hate what is evil; cling to what is good. Be devoted to one another in brotherly love. Honor one another above your-selves* (Rom. 12:9-10).

Do I really hate evil? Am I lovingly devoted to others? Are people who know me impressed by the way I honor others?

PRAYER—*Pray in the Spirit on all occasions with all kinds of prayers and requests. With this in mind, be alert and always keep on praying for all the saints* (Eph. 6:18).

Do I pray throughout each day with "all kinds of prayers"? Am I faithfully covering the Christians around me in prayer?

SPIRITUAL GIFTS—*Each one should use whatever [spiritual] gift he has received to serve others . . . so that in all things God may be praised through Jesus Christ* (1 Pet. 4:10-11).

Do I know my spiritual gifts? Am I using them to serve others?

GOD'S KINGDOM—*"Seek first [God's] kingdom and his righteousness, and all these things [needs of life] will be given to you as well"* (Matt. 6:33).

Am I investing my life in eternal things? Do my decisions reflect God's desires rather than my own?

THOUGHT CONTROL—*Whatever is true, whatever is noble, whatever is right, whatever is pure, whatever is lovely, whatever is admirable—if any-thing is excellent or praiseworthy—think about such things* (Phil. 4:8).

Do I normally think within these boundaries?

MY BODY—*Do you not know that your body is a temple of the Holy Spirit, who is in you? . . . Therefore honor God with your body* (1 Cor. 6:19-20).

Do I take good care of my body and avoid practices that defile or endanger it?

USE OF TIME—*Be . . . wise . . . making the most of every opportunity, because the days are evil* (Eph. 5:15-16).

Am I using my time in ways that count and that glorify the Lord?

APPENDIX H

Interceding for the Unsaved

Intercede for unsaved persons for . . .

SALVATION—*My heart's desire and prayer to God for the Israelites is that they may be saved* (Rom. 10:1).
Join with Paul in praying for the salvation of Jewish people. Ask God if there is some special nation for whom you should pray.

GOD'S DRAWING—*"No one can come to me unless the Father who sent me draws him"* (John 6:44).
Ask God to draw specific persons that you name. Pray that they will respond to God's drawing.

UNDERSTANDING—*"When anyone hears the message about the kingdom and does not understand it, the evil one comes and snatches away what was sown in his heart"* (Matt. 13:19).
Pray that those who hear the gospel will understand it.

OPEN EYES—*The god of this age has blinded the minds of unbelievers, so that they cannot see the light of the gospel of the glory of Christ* (2 Cor. 4:4).
Pray that unbelievers' eyes will be open so that they can see the light.

REPENTENCE—*The Lord . . . is patient with you, not wanting anyone to perish, but everyone to come to repentance* (2 Pet. 3:9).
Pray for unsaved family members, friends, neighbors, and coworkers to repent so that they will not perish.

FAITH—*"God so loved the world that he gave his one and only Son, that whoever believes in him shall . . . have eternal life"* (John 3:16).
Pray that many will believe and have eternal life.

NEW BELIEVERS—*"My prayer is not for [my disciples] alone. I pray also for those who will believe in me through their message"* (John 17:20).
Join Jesus in praying for the vast numbers, now estimated at 160,000 a day, that are coming into the kingdom. Pray for those yet to come.

Learning to Love to Pray Seminar

The *Learning to Love to Pray* seminar is a prayer-training event that deepens and recharges people's prayer lives and helps churches become "houses of prayer."

The seminar and the *Love to Pray* book complement each other. Much of the content is the same. Those who have used the devotional book find their prayer lives further deepened by attending the seminar. And those who attend the seminar find the book reinforcing and expanding what they have gained at the seminar.

The seminar will encourage and equip
- ◆ believers who want to learn to love to pray.
- ◆ pastors who want to ignite prayer in the local church.
- ◆ intercessors who want to develop their prayer ministry capabilities.

The Seminar in Brief

- ◆ **Time.** Six hours of prayer training given on a Saturday, or Friday evening and Saturday.
- ◆ **Location.** A conveniently located local church usually hosts the seminar.
- ◆ **Promotion.** The host church promotes the seminar to its own members and to other churches in the area.
- ◆ **Size.** The host church plans and promotes for 100 or more attendees. This is a goal, not a required number.
- ◆ **Cost.** Participants pay a modest registration fee. The host church covers the speaker's travel cost and provides refreshments for breaks.
- ◆ **Leaders.** A number of qualified seminar leaders are available to lead *Learning to Love to Pray* seminars for local churches or multichurch groups.

Direct questions about the seminar to:
Alvin VanderGriend at Alvin@harvestprayer.com
Phone: 360-354-5072 (Pacific Standard Time)